200 Years of the American Presidency: The 1989 Inaugural Story
ISBN 0-9622510-0-3

Produced in U.S.A.   Design by Frost & Associates   Final Artwork and Type by Donning Co., Publishers   Printed and Bound by Walsworth Publishing Co.

The inauguration of an American president is at once symbol and political reality. It is the fusion, in splendid ceremony, of these two qualities that create the significance of each inauguration.

Conducted in the very seat of national power, the inauguration celebrates a government established and empowered by the "consent of the governed." Attended by hundreds of thousands of private citizens and by all members of Congress, it suggests a nation united in a peaceful co-existence of political opponents.

Since the first inauguration, the ceremony has represented the orderly transfer of power and the institutional stability of the oldest democratic state. Each inauguration thereby imparts a sense of renewal and hope to the people of the United States and to foreign observers who view the American presidency as an example of a leadership assumed in peace and unscarred by violent dissension.

A presidential inaugural also speaks to us of a powerful and living history—of an enduring reality in which each of us participates. In the literal sense, the inauguration is an oath of office. The new president publicly pledges fidelity to a written and inviolable Constitution. It is the first and most vital act of a republic. It is our Constitution and the government's adherence to its precepts that assures us the possibility of all else: freedom, equality before the law, the separation of powers and the democratic process. The inauguration recalls to us and reaffirms these realities— realities that simultaneously bind and liberate us as symbol alone could not.

Message from the Co-Chairmen

"An inaugural, especially this bicentennial one, is a time for a renewal of the American spirit."

This year we celebrate the Bicentennial Presidential Inaugural—200 years of peaceful and orderly transition of power within our executive branch of government. This is a record of democratic stability unmatched anywhere in the world.

Thus, this year's inauguration of George Bush as our forty-first President follows in the grand and glorious tradition that began on April 30, 1789, when General George Washington took the solemn oath of office as our first President. Though history fails to record a particular "theme" of that first inaugural, it might well have been the one President Bush chose for his—peace, prosperity and independence. From George to George, as we say, the realization of these goals has remained the steadfast commitment of the citizens of the United States of America.

An inaugural is a time for renewal of the American spirit and commemoration of the American experience. In this century alone, we have known both peace and war, prosperity and depression, unity and division. Constant though the struggle has been, it has taught us an invaluable lesson about ourselves as a people—our supply of self-confidence, good will and resilience is inexhaustible. As President Bush is fond of saying, America is the last, best hope of mankind on earth.

An inaugural is also a time to look forward to the promise and challenge of the future, to set the tone for the presidency that is about to take charge of the destiny of the American people for the next four years. Thus, the 1989 inaugural has focused a great deal of attention on the children of America who are, after all, our future. We are proud to note that we scheduled more events tailored to our youth than has any previous inaugural.

Finally, we would like to pay tribute to the hundreds of people who have contributed their time and talent to produce a spectacular commencement of the Bush presidency in this grand inaugural tradition. We have been honored to work alongside them, and we hope that the spirit of this inaugural will lift us on our mission to ensure peace, prosperity and independence for all Americans.

Bobby Holt   **Penne Percy Korth**
Co-Chairmen
American Bicentennial Presidential Inaugural

To Preserve, Protect and Defend
The Constitution of the United States

by Warren E. Burger

Two hundred years ago, George Washington took the constitutional oath as first President at Federal Hall on Wall Street in New York on April 30, 1789. He had traveled by carriage for nearly eight days from Mount Vernon, Virginia. Martha stayed home from that hard trip.

On the balcony of Federal Hall, with Samuel Otis holding the Bible, Chancellor Livingston, the highest judicial officer of New York State, administered the oath of office prescribed by the Constitution in Article II, Sec. 1:

> "I do solemnly swear (or affirm) that I will faithfully execute the Office of President of the United States, and will to the best of my Ability, preserve, protect and defend the Constitution of the United States."

After taking the oath, the new President attended services at nearby St. Paul's Church.

In Philadelphia, after the draft of the Constitution was signed on September 17, 1787, Benjamin Franklin was asked, "What have you wrought?" His answer: "A republic, if you can keep it."

On January 20, 1989, George Bush was inaugurated as the forty-first President of the United States, and we respond to Franklin that we have kept what they wrought through 200 tumultuous years. Since George Washington took the first presidential oath, we have maintained and expanded individual freedoms and the opportunities that our ordered liberty nourishes.

Virginia, the largest, most powerful state, had ratified the Constitution by 89 to 79, Massachusetts by 187 to 168, New York by 30 to 27. The Constitution went into effect for nine states when New Hampshire ratified on June 21, 1788, but not until Rhode Island ratified by 34 to 32 in 1790 were all 13 states united under the new Constitution.

In the years before 1789, the Articles of Confederation held 13 independent, sovereign states together in "a firm league of friendship," but the new Constitution provided a central government which has continued under a written constitution longer than any system in all history. The magnitude of the step from a loose confederation to a new nation probably was not yet fully understood. In a sense, ratification of the Constitution was an act of faith by the people—faith in their leaders as well as in the Constitution itself.

George Washington, fully aware of how narrow was the victory of the new Constitution, was also conscious of the problem of making the new system work. But the wisdom of the people in the choice of the man who led Americans from the struggles at Trenton and Valley Forge to victory at Yorktown was soon to become clear. Legend has it that Washington had declined, as some suggested, to wear his full-dress uniform, but rather wore a rust-brown homespun suit—to encourage American textile industry development. In his inaugural speech, Washington acknowledged being "conscious of his own deficiencies." This was characteristic of the modest man who had questioned his own abilities to lead the Revolutionary armies. But it had a reassuring significance for those Americans who were apprehensive about a single chief executive as being too much like a monarch. Later, Washington was to pursue the concept of limited tenure in beginning the two-term tradition.

Our forty-first President, George Bush, faces problems undreamed of in 1789 either by those who wrote the Constitution or by our first President. All Americans—indeed all people—love freedom and want peace that will expand both freedom and opportunity everywhere in the world, and all must wish our new President well.

★ ★ ★ ★

Warren E. Burger, former Chief Justice of the Supreme Court, is Chairman of the Commission on the Bicentennial of the U.S. Constitution.

President Bush in Statuary Hall for the Inaugural Luncheon with the Rembrandt Peale portrait of George Washington behind him.

Reflections on Power
And the Presidency

by Byron Kennard

"*Our country is an extensive one. We must either then renounce the blessings of the Union, or provide an Executive with sufficient vigor to pervade every part of it.*"

—Governeur Morris,
at the Constitutional Convention

As a nation, we count among our blessings the fact that George Washington, the man, was the model for George Washington, the president. The framers of the Constitution, in conceiving and designing the office, couldn't help but picture the revered Revolutionary hero in the job.

Thus, thanks to Washington's reputation for blameless integrity, greater power was vested in the post than might have been the case otherwise. The American Revolution, after all, had been fought to curb the abuse of executive power. Having dislodged a king, citizens of the new republic were understandably wary of proposals to create a new almighty leader.

Washington assumed the presidency with a keen sense of the burdens imposed by great responsibility. Having steered the country through the tortuous course of revolution, he had encountered in full measure the human fallibility that can accompany talk of the common good.

As for glory, Washington had

tasted its full measure, too. He was at the time the most famous and admired individual in the world. Now this high esteem was to be gambled—and perhaps lost—on an unprecedented political experiment in self-government. George Washington might justifiably have rested on his laurels at Mount Vernon. Instead, he assumed the duties of President of the United States.

"*...he shall take care that the laws be faithfully executed...*"

—The Constitution, Article II

It fell to Abraham Lincoln to protect and enforce the basic law of the land, the Constitution itself, in the struggle to maintain the Union. Today, we view Lincoln as the epitome of leadership because he and his cause ultimately triumphed. But Lincoln, the "Savior of the Union," masks Lincoln the man and politician.

To fully measure his greatness, we must remember how rife with division was not only the federal union, but also Lincoln's own party. Never was a man more afflicted by political sectarianism and the ambitions of rivals and foes. Many of his own allies and appointees actively sought to undermine or displace his leadership—even while the war raged virtually at the outskirts of the capital city. Often, it seemed that

the president had no party at all in his corner.

Lincoln knew the challenges of the presidency full well, but, sadly, he was never to experience personally the glory that surrounds his name and memory.

"*The President shall be Commander in Chief of the Army and Navy of the United States...*"

—The Constitution, Article II

Harry S Truman, newly installed in the White House, presided over the final days of combat in World War II, and little of the victors' triumph was ascribed to him. But the full responsibility for concluding the war, including the momentous decision to employ atomic weapons, fell on his shoulders. Truman also suffered the unpopularity caused by tumultuous postwar transition when long-standing social problems, neglected during the war years, burst upon the nation like a flood.

But Harry Truman knew his mind and stuck to it, boasting that he never lost a night's sleep to a tough decision. Leaving the White House, he was counted among the least admired presidents of modern times. But time was on his side, as Truman predicted it would be. Fortunately, he lived long enough to re-enter the glow of public esteem, and there he remains in memory.

No president in our history has been more glorified than our first, George Washington, often depicted, as here, with nearly religious reverence.

8

> *"...he shall nominate, and by and with the Advice and Consent of the Senate, shall appoint Ambassadors, other public Ministers and Consuls...and all other officers of the United States, whose Appointments are not herein otherwise provided for..."*
>
> —The Constitution, Article II

The presidential power to appoint has probably been a burden to every man who ever held the office. Presidents are damned if they do and damned if they don't. As James K. Polk observed in his diary, "In every appointment which the President makes, he disappoints half a dozen applicants and their friends, who, actuated by selfish and sordid motives, will prefer any other candidate in the next election, while the person appointed attributes the appointment to his own superior merit and does not even feel obliged by it."

Many presidents have been ill-served—and some betrayed—by people they brought into government. On the other side of the ledger, however, is a glorious record of achievement in public service. The power to appoint also has been used to enlist eminent and able people in government service, equipping them for succession to the presidency.

The rigors of the presidency are clearly reflected in Lincoln's White House portrait, taken while the nation struggled in civil war.

Washington brought into the Cabinet Jefferson, who, in turn, brought Madison, who, in turn, brought Monroe. Later, Theodore Roosevelt brought in William Howard Taft; Woodrow Wilson brought in Franklin Roosevelt; and Warren Harding brought in Herbert Hoover.

> *"He shall have Power, by and with the Advice and Consent of the Senate, to make Treaties..."*
>
> —The Constitution, Article II

The most momentous news Thomas Jefferson received while he occupied the White House was that his representatives had signed a treaty whereby the United States would acquire from France the entire province of Louisiana. "This removes from us the greatest source of danger to our peace," Jefferson declared, proudly and correctly. This use of presidential power more than doubled the size of the nation in one swift maneuver. Jefferson's treaty with the French was greeted with virtually unanimous acclaim, marking the high point of his first Administration.

"...whilst to have been deemed worthy by a majority of the People of the United States to fill the office of Chief Magistrate of the Republic is an honor which ought to satisfy the aspirations of the most ambitious citizen, the period of his actual possession of its powers and performance of its duties is and must, from the nature of things, always be, to a right-minded man one of toilsome and anxious probation..."
—Martin Van Buren

If it were easy to make decisions, all presidents would be judged great by their countrymen and by the verdict of history. But, manifestly, almost by definition, presidential decisions are not easy. For presidents, the outcome is always uncertain, the stakes always high and the question always shrouded in logical perplexity and emotional confusion. And the questions come fast and furious, countless and inexorable. "The buck stops here," read the famous plaque on Harry Truman's Oval Office desk. The plaque has long since been removed, but the burden of responsibility still rests there, awaiting each new incumbent.

★ ★ ★ ★

Byron Kennard is a Washington, D.C.-based writer.

President Truman and his wife Bess on one of their campaign whistle stop tours.

President John F. Kennedy felt the weight of the office most oppressively during the Cuban Missile Crisis in 1962.

Texas Congressman Bush with former President Dwight D. Eisenhower.

Two Centuries of the American Presidency

by Clyde Linsley and Carl S. Anthony

The American presidency was, by any measure, a risky experiment. The founding fathers were aware of that, which may be why the Constitution left so many questions for future generations to answer.

The successful, worldly men who forged our government were acquainted with kings, with emperors, with military leaders, with statesmen, politicians, bureaucrats and citizens—and were skeptical of them all. None of them by themselves, they believed, were adequate to the task of governing a struggling young republic. What the nation needed at its head, they felt, was not one or the other but all of them at once: a man with the stature of a king who, unlike a king, served a fixed term at the will of the people, at the end of which he would return to the status of ordinary citizen. While in office he would be both the commander-in-chief of the nation's military forces and the man who operated the machinery of the civilian government as well.

Would these duties conflict? Probably. Could the conflicts be resolved? Perhaps. And what would result from this melange? Well, we would see.

And so we have. The 40 men who have held the presidency to date have all contributed to the definition of the office. George Herbert Walker Bush, the 41st, will do no less. The office has been defined, but the definition is not yet complete. There are surprises to come for those who hold the office in the future and for those of us who put them there.

We have experimented with the office over the past two centuries. The men we have chosen for the job have been southerners, northerners and, increasingly, westerners. They have been lawyers, engineers, generals and farmers. One was trained as a journalist; another had medical training. Some were essentially self-taught. None were young men as we understand the term today; the Constitution precludes it. They came to the job with the thought patterns, the understandings—and often the prejudices—of a lifetime.

What have they made of the office? What do we know about the presidency today, as a result of their having served in it? One thing seems clear: None

No president had a harder act to follow than John Adams, who succeeded George Washington as the nation's chief executive.

Andrew Jackson's presidency benefited from the fascination that Americans have for those who rise from humble beginnings.

14

Andrew Jackson

of them diminished it, although some had ample opportunity. The office was greater than they, and most of its occupants became greater for having been there.

The Job Requirements

One aspect of the presidency was clear from the beginning and has only been made clearer with the passage of time: It is a difficult job. "No easy matters will ever come to you," the fatherly Dwight D. Eisenhower advised his young successor, John F. Kennedy, on his inauguration. "If they're easy, they will be settled at a lower level."

No one knew better than Abraham Lincoln how difficult the job could be. He came to office presiding over a nation on the brink of dissolution, and within weeks of his inauguration, he was faced with a major decision guaranteed to ignite a civil war.

The state of South Carolina was prepared to wrest control of Fort Sumter from the federal government, and the fort was ill-equipped to defend itself. The fort sat on an island in Charleston Harbor. Reinforcements might save it, but it would be difficult to hold in the long run, and the mere act of sending reinforcements might be the final straw to the South. It would send a message to the South that the federal government would fight to prevent secession, and that message would make war inevitable.

Lincoln faced a choice between

war and capitulation. He reluctantly chose war. Reinforcements were ordered, but the fort was attacked before they could be deployed. Fort Sumter fell to the South, and the Civil War had begun.

But, of course, the story did not end there. Lincoln's decision failed to save Fort Sumter, but it may well have saved the Union. It united unionists and abolitionists, and it rallied those who had been wavering in their support. It clarified the issues of the struggle and gave a frightened nation the cour-

James K. Polk, one of our most successful and productive presidents, was also one of the least-known.

16

performs his duty faithfully...can have any leisure," he wrote. "If he entrusts the details...to subordinates, constant errors will occur. I prefer to supervise the whole operations of government myself, and this makes my duties very great."

Polk's vision of "Manifest Destiny" was fulfilled by the end of his term: He expanded the U.S. borders from the Southwest—a result of the Mexican War—to the Pacific—acquired by skillful diplomacy with England in a treaty for the Oregon territory. But though we are grateful today for his accomplishments, we seldom remember the man who achieved them. Polk died within three months of leaving office—one of the least-known presidents in history. It could be said that he failed to understand the symbolic and ceremonial aspects of leadership.

Squinting Toward Monarchy

Did the founding fathers understand the important ceremonial role that the president would play in our national life? Perhaps their first choice for the job shows that they did. George Washington, a majestic man who towered over most of his contemporaries, was made to order for ceremonial occasions. When Washington became president, Patrick Henry noted with concern, "It squints toward monarchy. Your president may easily become king."

Yet it was Washington's very

ge to persevere through difficult mes.

Workaholics do not seem) fare well in the presidency. imes K. Polk was one of those en nominated as a "dark horse" nd ran with the promise that he ould serve only one term. He stuck to his promise, and, in the course of his four years, worked daily late into the night. If he had to attend White House dinners, Polk would afterward return to his office, making up for the "lost hours" spent on what he considered frivolity. "No president who

The Garfield family at the White House. An able politician and formidable intellect, James Garfield is remembered in history as the second U.S. president to be assassinated.

17

conscious and precise balance between dignity and democracy that averted such a development. Acutely aware that his every action set precedents, Washington walked a fine line between upholding the dignity of the new office and maintaining the republican principles on which the new nation had been founded. The office—and the man who held it—would have respect, but there would be no Sun King in America.

Americans like it that way. Indeed, we seem to have a fascination with men from humble beginnings: Jackson, Lincoln, Lyndon Johnson, Ulysses S. Grant. The lure of the "man of the people" imagery is so strong that even the well-to-do have been known to adopt it. William Henry Harrison, born to wealth and high position as the grandson of a signer of the Declaration of Independence, was presented successfully to the electorate as the "log cabin and cider" candidate.

Virginia is proudly the "Mother of Presidents," with eight of its native sons elected to the office. Ohio contributed seven—all

▮
President Benjamin Harrison was escorted by a flotilla of boats across New York City harbor on April 30, 1889, in a gesture reminiscent of George Washington's own journey to Federal Hall where he took the first oath of office.

Republicans who served between 1869 and 1923. George Bush, John Adams, John Quincy Adams and John F. Kennedy were born in Massachusetts, and New York also produced four presidents: the two Roosevelts, Van Buren and Fillmore.

Every president until Lincoln was born and raised in the East, even "westerner" Andrew Jackson who, though elected from Tennessee, was born in South Carolina. Seven presidents were born in log cabins. Ulysses S. Grant's two-room birthplace was so revered that it was uprooted and placed on a riverboat as a traveling exhibit, after which it was displayed encased in glass.

Many presidents represent several states. Hoover was the first president born west of the Mississippi, in Iowa, but he lived in California and retired to New York. Eisenhower, born in Texas and raised in Kansas, was elected from New York and had a home in Pennsylvania.

Entangling Alliances

On leaving office, Washington warned the nation against becoming involved with "the insidious wiles of foreign influence." It was good advice for his day when the nation was small and weak and burdened with debt, but it was impossible to pursue in the long run. The United States was destined to play on the world stage, whether it wanted to or not.

In fact, destiny began calling almost immediately. John Adams inherited an ongoing dispute with France when he succeeded Washington in 1797. As a result of the dispute, the United States found itself in an informal alliance with Great Britain.

Alliances shifted and reformed over the following decades. By 1814, President James Madison was fleeing the capital as British soldiers ransacked the city and burned the White House.

The War of 1812 demonstrated that the nation required a strong defense. As James Monroe prepared to take office succeeding Madison as the fifth president, Congress enacted legislation increasing the size of the standing army and appropriating funds for 15 new battleships.

Monroe did not shy from foreign relations. He worked to strengthen relations with the British in Canada and, with his secretary of state, John Quincy Adams, issued the Monroe Doctrine, which served notice that the United States intended to play a leadership role in the affairs of the Western Hemisphere.

Despite occasional flirtations with isolationism, American presidents have considered foreign relations one of their most important duties. Theodore Roosevelt

William Taft initiated what has almost become a tradition—the golf-playing president.

Always conscious of his public image, "Teddy" Roosevelt is pictured here on one of his hunting trips.

used his power to strengthen the nation's presence in the Americas and the Caribbean, and he played a greater role than any of his predecessors in maintaining a balance of power in the Pacific. After World War II, Harry S Truman was instrumental in the rebuilding of war-ravaged Europe.

Many presidents have achieved their most enduring accomplishments in foreign policy. John F. Kennedy attacked starvation, poverty and disease around the world with his Peace Corps and Alliance for Progress. Richard Nixon achieved detente with the Soviet Union and rapprochement with China; these proved to be among his most historic accomplishments. Jimmy Carter's personal determination to bring peace to the Mideast resulted in the Camp David Accords between Egypt and Israel. Ronald Reagan's ambition to halt the dangerously accelerating arms race with the Soviet Union was realized by his INF (Intermediate Nuclear Forces) Treaty.

But a president ignores domestic responsibilities at his peril, for it is often what happens at home, on his own ground, that influences an American voter most. Franklin D. Roosevelt could not have ignored the effects of the Great Depression and hoped to retain his office. Through programs such as the Works Progress Administration, FDR managed to show that the resources of government could be put to work to solve

acute national problems, and his regular radio fireside chats demonstrated that the president could serve as an inspirational, morale-building figure in times of trouble.

The President and the Public

A president must be in touch with the people he represents. Jefferson initiated a Fourth of July reception on the lawn for the general public and—until the sheer numbers finally prevented it during Hoover's term—all presidents since George Washington held a New Year's Day open house for the public. Hoover said a president's decisions affected "the happiness of every home."

The public and the press have always glorified and vilified the man in a moment's notice. Early political cartoons cruelly portrayed Jefferson as a Francophile, Van Buren as a trickster, Buchanan as a Confederate sympathizer and Lincoln as a buffoon.

Presidents have long nurtured a love-hate relationship with the press, reveling in the public exposure but seething at the criticism that often accompanies it.

A woman newspaper correspondent once followed President John Quincy Adams down to the banks of the Potomac, waited until he had disrobed for his predawn swim and then sat on his clothes until he consented to answer her questions.

Theodore Roosevelt was the first to befriend journalists by

providing an official news room after seeing them huddled outside in the cold, but Wilson recognized their increasing importance to the presidency as a means of getting word out to the populace. He held the first presidential press conference.

Harding entered the presidency stating that he hoped to be "the best-loved president." One of the few pleasures he found in the role was being able to chat with the public. Daily, he set one hour aside to welcome groups and individuals, from factory workers to scientists. Calvin Coolidge willingly appeared for the machines of the "moving picture" cameras, the first president to appear in silent newsreels, which were shown to the public between feature films in theaters. Truman was the first to address the nation on television.

The advent of electronic communications has influenced the nature of the presidency itself. Today the president learns of events around the world more quickly than Lincoln did about events at Gettysburg, and he can respond nearly as fast. This accelerated pace puts considerable pressure on the president and makes sober reflection far more difficult.

Riding the Tiger

The president is never off duty. He may take a vacation, but the responsibilities of the job go with him. So does a retinue of aides

and support staff. A man can go trout fishing by himself, but a man who is president must go with an army of people and a battery of sophisticated communications equipment.

Nor can he entertain privately. When you are the president, every function is a public occasion. The guest list for a White House dinner is read as avidly in Washington, D.C., as the latest assessment of military might around the world or the Department of Agriculture's newest crop forecasts.

A president's every action sends a message to the nation

about his administration. Jefferson liked to use oval tables for dinner, not for style so much as for its democratic representation: Everyone was equal in the round. When Theodore Roosevelt welcomed the eminent Booker T. Washington to lunch, it was more than a meal: It broke precedent as the first time a black man was invited to dine with a president. The Kennedys' guest list included poets, painters, playwrights and musicians, and it sent a public message of presidential respect for the arts.

Harry Truman quipped, "Being

a president is like riding a tiger. A man has to keep on riding or be swallowed."

Nevertheless, recreation is essential if he is to retain his sanity and health, and presidents have resorted to a variety of recreational activities. Harry Truman enjoyed a game of horseshoes on the South Lawn, and Theodore Roosevelt's mile-long strides at dawn are part of the legend. Grant was an expert horseman, and Benjamin Harrison frequently hunted game. Eisenhower was perhaps the nation's most famous golfer, but Woodrow Wilson was

almost as devoted to the links.

Herbert Hoover, who established the first official presidential retreat, explained that leisure was a necessary part of being president, "for refreshment of one's soul and clarification of one's thoughts."

Steward of the People

"It is the duty of the president," Theodore Roosevelt emphatically stated, "to act upon the theory that he is the steward of the people."

It is in many ways a makeshift existence, to live for four years or more, at your country's beck and call, in a house that is not your own, under the unblinking gaze of the media and the public, your every utterance recorded for posterity, and with the fate of the world on your shoulders.

It is a difficult burden, but it is also, as Thomas Jefferson called it, a "glorious burden," and it exercises a tremendous hold on our imagination. The presidency is an opportunity for a man—or woman—to leave an indelible impression on history. Few receive such an opportunity, and few who receive it would pass it by.

It is a prize well worth seeking.

As Woodrow Wilson said, a president is at liberty to be "as big a man as he can. His capacity will set the limit."

★ ★ ★ ★

Clyde Linsley is a Virginia-based writer. Carl Sferrazza Anthony assisted in the research for this article.

George Washington takes the presidential oath administered by New York Chancellor Robert R. Livingston on April 30, 1789, at New York City Federal Hall.

Constructed in the 1790s, the White House was completed in time for our second president, John Adams, to occupy it in 1800.

Milestones of the American Presidency

President James Monroe delivered his statement on American foreign policy that became known as the Monroe Doctrine.

Under the administration of President John Quincy Adams, the Canal Era dawned in America, rapidly expanding commerce.

1817

1825

1801

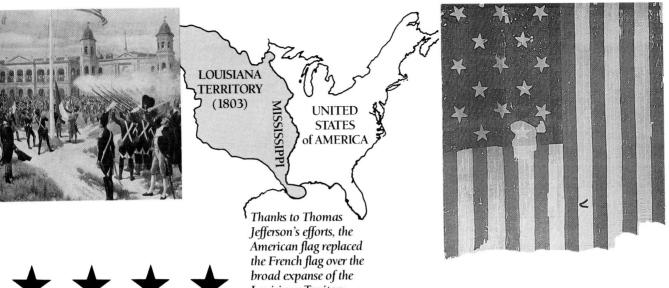

LOUISIANA TERRITORY (1803)

MISSISSIPPI

UNITED STATES of AMERICA

Thanks to Thomas Jefferson's efforts, the American flag replaced the French flag over the broad expanse of the Louisiana Territory.

1809

The original "Star Spangled Banner" American flag that flew over Fort McHenry during the War of 1812 inspired Francis Scott Key to pen the poem that became our national anthem.

★ ★ ★ ★

Our seventh president, Andrew Jackson, was the first to ride a railroad train as demonstrated here by the famous John Bull steam engine.

1829

In the same year that Martin Van Buren was elected president, proud Texans defended the Alamo, and the Republic of Texas was on its way to becoming the Lone Star State.

1837

1841

William Henry Harrison died in office after serving only one month as president; the succession of the vice president to chief executive was established.

★ ★ ★ ★

1841

During John Tyler's presidency, Samuel F. C. Morse demonstrated his invention of the "Morse Code" in a room at the U.S. Capitol, revolutionizing communications.

1845

While James K. Polk was president, the U.S. borders were extended to the Pacific Ocean, gold was discovered in California and the "Gold Rush" began.

Pennsylvania's only president, James Buchanan, welcomed the first Japanese envoys to the White House.

In the midst of the Civil War, Abraham Lincoln delivered his immortal Gettysburg Address in tribute to the most tragic of the war's battles.

Andrew Johnson became the first and only president to be impeached under the constitutional amendment providing for removal of a chief executive. Shown here is a ticket to his impeachment trial that resulted in Johnson's acquittal.

1857

1861

1865

1849

Under the presidency of Zachary Taylor, the question of whether new states should enter the Union as "free" or "slave" was debated; California, its state flag displaying a bear, entered as a free state.

1850

The first trade expedition to Japan, led by Admiral Matthew Perry, set sail from the United States while Millard Fillmore was president.

1853

Franklin Pierce, a northerner with southern sympathies, pictured here with his Cabinet that included both northerners and southerners, had to deal with increasingly violent sectional strife such as "Bloody Kansas," a result of the Kansas-Nebraska Act.

During Ulysses S. Grant's second term as president, the United States celebrated its centennial at an exposition in Philadelphia. Here, at the opening ceremony, Grant is about to start the great Corliss engine, which symbolically set the celebration in motion.

1869

Rutherford B. Hayes welcomed the first official envoys from the Chinese Empire.

1877

During the term of James Garfield, Tuskegee Institute was founded; it was there that scientist George Washington Carver performed many of his extraordinary experiments.

29

1881

1881

President Chester Alan Arthur came from Washington, D.C., to dedicate the Brooklyn Bridge in 1884. The bridge is still considered an engineering wonder of the world.

1885

Grover Cleveland not only took the oath of office as president in 1885, but also in 1893, making him the only U.S. president to serve two non-consecutive terms.

1889

Benjamin Harrison, the grandson of President William Henry Harrison, used his famous relative's campaign slogan and paraphernalia ("Keep the Ball Rolling") for his own campaign in 1888. Under his term, the Oklahoma Territory was opened for settlement.

William Howard Taft was the first president to throw out a baseball to open the baseball season.

1909

Woodrow Wilson played a vital role in the Versailles peace talks following World War I.

1913

Warren G. Harding was the first president to travel to the Territory of Alaska.

1921

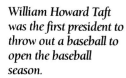

1897

William McKinley served as president during the short, but hard-fought Spanish-American War and shepherded its peace treaty through Congress.

1901

Theodore Roosevelt promoted conservation, a strengthened modern navy, fair labor laws, "trust-busting," and food and drug standards. He also encouraged the government's use and purchase of airplanes, and he became the first president to travel by "flying machine."

Calvin Coolidge was not only the first president to regularly pose for newsreels, but also the first to make frequent speeches via radio.

Of all our presidents, Franklin D. Roosevelt gave the greatest access to the press corps throughout his 12 years in office.

1923

Herbert Hoover welcomed Amelia Earhart, the first woman to fly solo across the Atlantic, to the White House after her return.

1929   **1933**

1945

Harry Truman ended World War II by ordering atomic bombs dropped on Hiroshima and Nagasaki.

1953

Dwight D. Eisenhower took part in the first Geneva Conference, with British, French and Soviet leaders.

Gerald Ford, here meeting with his National Security Council advisers, ordered the evacuation of Americans from Vietnam, a war that began four administrations earlier.

1974

Jimmy Carter not only brought Israel and Egypt together for a peace accord, but he also became the first president to welcome a pope to the White House.

1976

hn F. Kennedy appointed the first Special
dvisory Council on the Arts, and with his wife
cqueline, focused national attention on cultural
sues. Here, the Kennedys attend the premier
chibition of the famous Mona Lisa, which was
aned to the United States by France.

1963

Lyndon Baines Johnson signed the Civil Rights
Act in 1964 and began social programs that
improved the standard of living for many
Americans.

1969

Richard M. Nixon promoted the well-
being of the earth by founding the
Environmental Protection Agency and
was also a devoted advocate of space
exploration. While he was president,
Apollo 11 carried the first men to land
on the moon.

Ronald Reagan alleviated "Cold War" tensions
by fostering a positive relationship with Soviet
President Mikhail Gorbachev. Here the two
leaders sign the historic INF Treaty in 1987.

On their last morning in the White House, President and Mrs. Reagan wait to greet the new residents.

As the Marine helicopter takes a final spin around the Capitol, former President Ronald Reagan bids farewell.

Passing the Torch

by Timothy P. O'Neill

"The world is quiet today, Mr. President." With those words, National Security Adviser Colin Powell delivered his final

report to President Ronald Reagan shortly before noon, January 20, 1989. Thus reassured, the 40th president prepared for the end of his eight-year watch, which would take place at precisely 12:05 p.m. when George Bush uttered the now-familiar 35-word oath of office on the steps of the Capitol. With that simple pledge "to preserve, protect and defend the Constitution of the United States," Mr. Bush became our 41st president and Mr. Reagan became a private citizen.

In this fashion, the torch of the presidency has been passed since 1789 when George Washington first repeated the oath at Federal Hall in New York City. This orderly transfer of power prescribed by the Constitution has been one constant in 200 years of change. During this time span, the United States has evolved from a sparsely populated, underdeveloped agrarian nation into a highly centralized and technologically advanced superpower.

Yet the Constitution has endured. Indeed, this blueprint for democratic, republican government was drafted so wisely and well that throughout our history it has been subject to amendment only 26 times. It could be argued with some force that it is precisely the political stability bestowed by our constitutional framework that has powered America's rise to greatness and given vision and hope to the poor and oppressed around the world. Our affluence, inventiveness and power are all truly impressive, but our Constitution and the system of government it called into being are America's greatest gifts to mankind.

The presidency, of course, is an integral part of that system, and in 1989 we celebrate the 200th anniversary of the executive branch of government. The procession of presidencies from Washington's first inaugural has been orderly, though not always serene. Presidents have taken the oath in a variety of circumstances, in the midst of civil war and world war, upon the natural deaths of their predecessors, and in the wake of assassinations. Presidents have taken their oath in a variety of places as well—in the rotunda of the Capitol, on the porch of the White House, a Vermont farmhouse, a New York City brownstone and on board a jet plane. Yet no catastrophe has been so great as to disrupt the constitutional order.

In attempting to understand the essence of the presidency, it is instructive to note that the oath of office requires a pledge to defend not the people of the United States, *but the Constitution of the United States* against all enemies, foreign and domestic. We elect our president to see that our laws are faithfully executed, but within constitutional limits.

The president is assuredly not a monarch. For irrefutable evidence of the correctness of this proposition, we need look no further than the traditional inaugural ceremony itself. As has already been noted, the oath is taken by the new president to defend the Constitution, thus placing "the laws above the prince." Presidential deference to the other two coequal branches of government is symbolized by where the oath is taken (the steps of the Capitol that houses the Congress) and by whom the oath is administered (the Chief Justice of the Supreme Court of the United States). Thus the vitality of our tripartite system of government, not just the executive branch, is celebrated in the inauguration of a new president. That it is a public ceremony, traditionally held outdoors and witnessed by thousands of citizens, is significant as well. For the presidential power that is transferred at an inauguration is power to be exercised by the "consent of the governed."

The inaugural ceremony is the most visible affirmation we make of our faith in our institutions and ourselves. Private citizen Ronald Reagan quietly spoke to the troops at Andrews Air Force Base as he reviewed them one last time: "Just carry on." And so we will.

★ ★ ★ ★

Timothy P. O'Neill is a Washington, D.C.-based writer who has been a speech writer for Dan Quayle and Sen. Nancy Kassenbaum.

The final salute, the passing of the torch completed, former President Reagan leaves the future in capable hands.

George Bush

by Victor Gold

"I always want to hear the other person's point of view—provided, of course, that I get a chance to express my own. Even if you don't change anybody's mind, it clears the air and gets both sides seeing each other as human beings."

George Bush
Looking Forward: An Autobiography

January 20, 1969, Inaugural Day, 20 years ago. A brisk wind swept down Pennsylvania Avenue, from the White House to the Capitol, where a new president would be sworn in at noon. Congressman George Bush was about to leave his Longworth Building office, headed for the parade review stands, when a member of his staff suggested a change in schedule.

"You really don't need to sit in the cold for three hours," said Rose Zamaria, the Congressman's office manager. "What you ought to do is go out to Andrews and say goodbye to President Johnson, to wish him well. He's a Democrat, but he's a fellow Texan, and he's been our President."

George Bush thought about that suggestion a mere moment, then headed not for the review stands but for Andrews Air Force Base, where members of Lyndon Johnson's Cabinet, along with a handful of his friends from the Senate and House, were lined up to say their farewells.

"It turned out I was the only Republican there," Bush later recalled. "The President went down the line, his face masking whatever thoughts he had on leaving the city where he'd spent the greater part of his life. Hard as I'd worked against the man over the years—not Johnson personally, but his policies—I couldn't help but feel the poignancy of the moment.…I shook his hand and wished him a safe journey. He nodded, took a few steps toward the ramp, then turned, looked back at me, and said, 'Thanks for coming.'"

There is no need to search any further than this vignette from an Inaugural Day past to find the key to our forty-first President's approach to governance and politics. The process, for George Bush, is about ideas, but not ideas in the cold abstract. First and foremost, it's about people.

As George Bush sees it, leadership in a free society begins with hearing other people out, listening, *then* making a decision. He believes in keeping "an open door and an open mind," in the style of one of his favorite predecessors in the Oval Office, Theodore Roosevelt.

It was from a maxim followed by the irrepressible "Teddy"— whose portrait will grace the wall of the Bush White House Cabinet Room—that our new President took the title of his autobiography: "Look up and not down; look out and not in; look forward and not back; and lend a hand."

That was the credo of Roosevelt's "Bull Moose" party in 1912, one reflecting the spirit of confident optimism that infused the American people in the early years of the twentieth century. Seventy-seven years later, it reflects the spirit of the self-defined optimist chosen to lead America into the decade of the 1990s.

George Herbert Walker Bush will come to the White House as one of the best-prepared presidents in modern history, having traveled, in the two decades since he left Congress, a road that led to New York, as U.S. ambassador to the United Nations; back to Washington, as chairman of the Republican National Committee; to Beijing, as America's envoy to the People's Republic of China; to Langley, as director of the Central Intelligence Agency; and to the rambling Victorian residence on Observatory Circle where, for the past eight years, he has served as Ronald Reagan's loyal vice-president.

George Bush is a man on the move, yet one of fixed and abiding values. The White House, its new occupant feels, "can set the tone, an atmosphere, a standard for the nation." And more: "As President," George Bush has written, "I mean to work toward a new harmony, a greater tolerance, an understanding that this country is a partnership—a partnership bound together not for the mere pursuit of material gain, but by a shared faith."

It is a shared faith in freedom and the future, as we move toward a new decade and a new century, a faith tested and proven in the crucible of the American experience as well as that of our forty-first President.

★ ★ ★ ★

Victor Gold is co-author of George Bush's autobiography, Looking Forward: An Autobiography.

■
*The future president
reviews his inaugural
address in the courtyard
of Blair House.*

42

Barbara Bush

by Victor Gold

Barbara Bush isn't going to change. She is the same beautiful young woman who left Rye, New York, 43 years ago to make her way in the world as the life-partner of Lieutenant George Bush, USN. She is funny, self-effacing, somewhat wiser perhaps, but in spirit and outlook, not a day older.

On a bright, chill day in mid-December, five weeks after her husband had been elected President, the First Lady-to-be sipped coffee in the living room of the vice president's residence that she and George had lived in for eight years and fretted. No, that's not quite the right word: Barbara Bush isn't the fretting kind. When something troubles her, she *braces* the problem and takes it head-on, especially when it involves George and the family.

How, she wondered, was George's new job going to affect the lives of the Bush children?

Barbara Bush has had to ask that question many times during the past 40 years. How would the children's lives be affected when their father became ambassador to the United Nations? Became U.S. envoy to Beijing? Became head of the CIA? Vice president? A candidate for president?

The jobs have always been challenging and being the life-partner of George Bush has always been exhilarating, but Barbara Bush never forgets her personal priorities. Public life, yes, but never at the price of family life.

True, the five Bush children—George Jr., Jeb, Neil, Marvin and Dorothy—aren't exactly children anymore. They're all grown, with children of their own. Not only grown, but independent and self-reliant, qualities very much a part of the Bush family formula for bringing up children. Love and independence, says Barbara Bush, are two sides of the same coin: Didn't she and George in their early twenties leave loving parents to move to Texas and shape lives of their own?

> *"She is a hip, funny lady, her humor self-deprecating and wise. She is stoic, forceful and motherly, bearing the admirable traits of aristocracy. But more than anything else, she is content, nearly enchanted, to be the wife of George Bush and the mother of their children."*
>
> **Christopher Rose**
> New Orleans *Times-Picayune*

For George, that meant life in the oil fields, building a business to provide for a growing family, followed by a career of public service. For Barbara, it meant life

as a strong, supportive wife and mother, then time given to community service. Neil's early problems with dyslexia led to her interest in programs to help children with reading disabilities and the national campaign to stamp out illiteracy. The tragic death of daughter Robin just before her fourth birthday drew Barbara into volunteer work for the Leukemia Society of America and Children's Oncology Services. A commitment to higher education, going back to the days when George headed campus fund-raising efforts for the United Negro College Fund, led to her membership on the board of Morehouse School of Medicine in Atlanta.

Busy days, a fulfilling life. But for Barbara Bush, it all comes back to home and the family. The address may change, but the home never does. Since the day in 1948 when she, George and George Jr. moved into that wood-frame duplex on a muddy street in Odessa, Texas, there have been more than two dozen changes in address. The eight years the Bushes have lived in the vice president's residence are the most they've spent in any house since George and Barbara were married.

And now there will be another house, making it 29 in all. How, Barbara Bush wanted to know, would this new move affect their five children—and the 10 Bush grandchildren? She took a sip of

coffee, shook her head, then asked, "Did you read what Doro had to say about it? She said her parents weren't going to let the White House give their kids a big head."

The First Lady-to-be put down her coffee cup, then smiled. "She's right, too," she said. "We're not going to let that happen. You can count on it."

Barbara Bush. The same young Barbara Bush. Living in a wood-frame duplex on a muddy street in Odessa, Texas, or as First Lady of the Land, she hasn't changed. She doesn't plan to change. Just ask George or their children. They are counting on it.

★ ★ ★ ★

Victor Gold is co-author of George Bush's autobiography, Looking Forward: An Autobiography.

President and Mrs. Bush pose with their family, at the White House. Back row, from left, Bill LeBlond, Doro Bush LeBlond, Neil Bush, Sharon Bush, Marshall Bush, Columbia Bush, Marvin Bush, Jeb Bush, George Bush, and Laura Bush. Children behind the president, Jenna and Barbara Bush, Noelle and George Bush. On the couch, from left, Lauren and Pierce Bush, Mrs. Bush, Jebby Bush, the President, Ellie and Sam LeBlond, and Margaret Bush.

■
*One of the Bush twins,
Barbara, shares a secret
with her grandmother
at the Inaugural Gala.*

▬
*The Bushes enjoy an
afternoon in Kenne-
bunkport with their
grandchildren.*

◧
*A rare opportunity to
share some solitude
together.*

Dan Quayle

by Kenneth Adelman

Indiana folks know Dan Quayle best of all. That's why, after giving him an upset win in 1980, Hoosiers reelected him to the U.S. Senate in 1986 with what was then the largest margin of any state-wide candidate in this century.

Hoosiers saw in Dan Quayle a man of character, a family man who would forego Washington's social whirl to spend evenings and weekends with his wife, Marilyn, and their three children—Tucker, Ben and Corinne. They saw a man who could find time in his busy Senate schedule to coach his son's basketball team.

The times Dan Quayle and I have spent together over the years have largely been times with our families—swimming, bowling, hiking, playing touch football or just hanging around our house or theirs. Dinners together have been family dinners; sports were comprised of family teams; vacations were always family outings.

Hoosiers appreciated the fact that their popular young Senator focused on two areas most critical to their future: jobs and security.

They were proud that Dan Quayle assumed the leadership role in writing and pushing through America's innovative job training bill. He pulled along a skeptical business community to turn around the government's make-work public sector job program. His efforts placed disadvantaged and dislocated workers in tax-paying rather than

tax-consuming positions. He helped put Americans back on the payroll after a demeaning time on the welfare roll.

Hoosiers knew that more than 70 percent of 4 million adults

went into private sector jobs after completing their job training. Years after the bill was passed, an editorial in the *Wall Street Journal* commended Quayle's legislation as "indeed a success. Tens of

thousands of hard-core unemployed today have the skills to find and keep a job. The cost of the federal bureaucracy has been reduced."

The solid people of Indiana know that Quayle was key to the Senate's improving, and then approving, the first arms control treaty to eliminate an entire class of nuclear weapons. He worked tirelessly for an arms control agreement that advanced, rather than eroded, America's strength. We in the U.S. Arms Control and Disarmament Agency knew amendments would not have happened without his dedication and knowledge.

Hoosiers also saw that while insistent on a robust defense, Quayle pushed for reforms in Pentagon purchasing long before it became fashionable. He worked closely with Senate Democrats in a bipartisan spirit, living the words of the late Senator Henry "Scoop" Jackson: "On matters of national security, the best politics is no politics."

"Dan Quayle symbolizes the future—optimistic, patriotic and dedicated."

Time and again over the years of our professional association and friendship, I have seen Dan Quayle's inquisitive mind at work. He constantly peppers anyone around with questions on topics

ranging from defense procurement to deployment in the Persian Gulf. He always wants to know more, on almost any subject, almost all the time.

And he devours books with a voraciousness all too rare among practicing politicians. In late summer, I sent him a book on educational reform for his "recreational reading." The next time I was at his house, he tossed it back, starting to discuss what he'd read. I hemmed and hawed, delaying the conversation until I'd had a chance to read it, too.

Hoosiers sense that Dan Quayle symbolizes the future. Optimistic, patriotic and dedicated, he epitomizes qualities they cherish most. George Bush said that Quayle "captures that young spirit that I think of" as characterizing his party and our nation.

What the people of Indiana knew first, George Bush knew as well. Now, over the next four years, the American people will become more familiar with Dan Quayle—a good man, a serious man, a fine American.

People across the nation will find that Hoosier judgment here, as elsewhere, is right on the mark.

★ ★ ★ ★

Kenneth Adelman, former director of the U.S. Arms Control and Disarmament Agency, is a nationally syndicated columnist.

■
Dan and Marilyn
Quayle greet children
on the campaign trail.

Marilyn Quayle

by Lynne V. Cheney

Marilyn Quayle had planned to resume the practice of law in 1989. After 11 years at home with her children, she—like so many women today—was going to combine motherhood and a career.

And she still is—except the career is not quite the one she had expected. Being married to any politician is a demanding and complicated enterprise; being married to the Vice President of the United States lifts responsibilities and complexities into a whole new realm.

During the 1988 campaign, Marilyn Quayle showed that she has what it takes to deal with the unexpected. She was, time and again, resourceful and unflappable. Consider the day she was to be interviewed by Barbara Walters. Marilyn had spent all day at state fairs, shaking hands, making polite and intelligent conversation—no easy challenge when you are meeting and greeting hundreds. It had been a long, hot day, and she was looking forward to changing clothes and combing her hair when she arrived at the television studio. But the clothes weren't there. Not even the comb was there. In the chaos typical of campaigns, her suitcase had been misdirected.

So Marilyn Quayle made do. She used Barbara Walters' comb and lipstick and went on nationwide television looking as fresh as a June morning in Indiana. Listening to her calm and reasoned answers to Barbara Walters' questions, no one would have guessed the kind of day she had experienced.

Marilyn Tucker met Dan Quayle 16 years ago. She was a bright young law student who, since childhood, had loved excelling. She had repeatedly proved herself capable of it, earning awards and honors beginning early in her grade school years. Having learned from her parents—both doctors—that achievement involves hard work, Marilyn Tucker was working steadily at a job in the state attorney general's office during the day and studying law at Indiana University at night. It was during this time that she encountered a handsome young man from Huntington who was also working days and going to law school at night. Ten weeks after they met, Marilyn Tucker and Dan Quayle were married by the law school dean.

Two years later, the Quayles' first son, Tucker, was born. A few days after the birth, his mother passed the bar examination.

Mrs. Bush and Mrs. Quayle offer each other a toast during the Congressional Luncheon in Statuary Hall.

Marilyn and Dan opened a law office together in Huntington, and by 1976 their practice was beginning to thrive. Then, Dan was elected to Congress, Benjamin Quayle was born, and Marilyn decided to suspend her career.

"Trying to find someone to care for two small children, traveling back and forth between Washington and Indiana, worrying about conflicts of interest—it just got to be too much," says Marilyn.

After a third child, Corinne, was born, Marilyn began to devote much of her formidable energy to her children's schools, where she has done everything from directing a Shakespeare play to coaching a baseball team. She joined study groups and gained a reputation for public speaking. And she remained a strong partner in a strong marriage.

"When you start out as equals, you stay that way," she says. Her husband frequently pays tribute to her savvy political instincts—and to her. "Marilyn is my best adviser, my strongest supporter and the person I love more than anyone in this world," he says.

It's not yet clear how Marilyn Quayle will define her new career, but she has gained the nation's attention and respect and will bring both to whatever causes she chooses to make her own. A woman of grace and grit, she will do well. Marilyn Quayle will, once again, excel.

★ ★ ★ ★

Lynne V. Cheney is chairman of the National Endowment for the Humanities.

■
On the campaign trail the Quayles celebrate Ben's birthday.

■
On their first morning in the Vice President's residence, the entire family relaxes with their guests.

■
Following their departure from the Capitol Hill luncheon, the Quayle family walk down Pennsylvania Avenue.

Inaugural

Week 1989

Inaugural Week 1989

by Clyde Linsley

*T*he nation celebrated as a new president began his term . . . and the American presidency began its third century.

A light snow had dusted the Washington area in early January, inevitably recalling to the minds of inaugural organizers the events of 1985, when blasts of wintry air swept through the region, forcing the swearing-in ceremony indoors to the Capitol rotunda and leading to cancellation of the Inaugural Parade. As the 1989 inaugural preparations proceeded and members of the armed forces strung snow fencing on the National Mall, those memories must have been an added concern.

But 1989 was not 1985. This year, the weather cooperated.

Although inauguration day was blustery, sunshine broke through the clouds and warmed the throngs of people gathered before the West Front of the Capitol building, waiting to hear George Herbert Walker Bush say the words that every president since Washington has said:

"I do solemnly swear that I will faithfully execute the office of President of the United States, and will to the best of my Ability, preserve, protect and defend the Constitution of the United States."

That was the climax of a week of festivities, but it was not the beginning, nor the sum. And, as has been the case with every

inauguration since Washington's, getting there was half the fun.

The Preparations

Inaugural week really began before the official opening celebration. As supporters and well-wishers streamed into Washington, D.C., from across the nation, the city worked overtime to receive and accommodate them.

The president-elect had a large extended family, and relatives from throughout the country

descended on the capital city to attend the inaugural events. Of the 100 rooms in the Jefferson Hotel, 90 were occupied by family members. As a major participant on the national political scene for several decades, the new president had made many friends and acquaintances who came to enjoy the inaugural experience. Airports, Union Station and hotel lobbies teemed with people who had come for the big occasion.

Rehearsals went ahead for the

Finishing touches are put on all inaugural activities during marathon countdown meetings conducted by Executive Director Stephen Studdert.

The afternoon before the inaugural parade, the future president reviews the route with his assistant, Andy Card.

big celebration with volunteers from the Armed Forces Inaugural Committee standing in for the principals. Army specialist Cliff Owens and Pfc. Margie Jiminez played President-elect and Mrs. Bush, striding down the carpeted runway at the Capitol building and waving to the non-existent crowds. "Now I know how the other half lives," Owens later told *The Washington Post*.

An inauguration is a major logistical exercise. Without countless rehearsals and countdown meetings, an event of this magnitude might never happen. On inauguration day, the new president visited 13 sites in the city. The Inaugural Parade included 211 marching units, floats and bands. The inaugural events required the services of more than 200 volunteer florists from 35 states, who created 1,500 floral arrangements to grace tables and archways.

Wednesday, January 18, 1989

The official inaugural activities began Wednesday, January 18, at the Lincoln Memorial. The opening celebration was free to the public.

About 40,000 people were present by the time the celebration got under way. The *Post* reported that Sugar Bratten of Harlingen, Texas, drove 36 straight hours with her husband and son to attend the inaugural. Other spectators were people who worked downtown and

opped off on their way home to atch the show. Some came out of curiosity; others may simply ave decided it was easier than egotiating the gridlock around ie Lincoln Memorial.

It was a big show. The Beach oys and The Gatlin Brothers layed and sang, as did Lee reenwood, Sandi Patti and Up Vith People; the U.S. Army olden Knights Parachute Team ropped in—literally—and 21 avy fighter planes flew overhead 1 a salute to the incoming resident.

At the end, President-elect ush lit a gas torch on the plat- orm. Then he and his family, ice President-elect Quayle and is family, and thousands of pectators turned on tiny flash- ghts, which had been passed ut to members of the audience s they entered.

"What is it that makes these 1ousands of points of light nine?" asked President-elect ush, echoing a theme from his lection campaign. "It's you."

The sky erupted with fireworks. 16-minute display was accom- anied by a recording of the oston Pops playing Aaron Cop- nd's "Fanfare for the Common lan."

But the evening wasn't over. bout 3,000 guests went on to ine at one of the three black-tie iaugural Dinners held around ie city: the Pension Building, nion Station and the Corcoran allery of Art.

The president-elect, vice

president-elect and their wives went to each dinner in turn, where guests were served a menu reminiscent of the first inaugural dinner, featuring favorites such as roast veal, corn souffle and Apple Cranberry Brown Betty.

At Constitution Hall, a tradi- tional venue for inaugural activi- ties, other inaugural guests were attending the first performance of the American Presidential Pageant, which was performed again several times during the week. Host Lee Greenwood helped a large cast, including members of the U.S. Army's Third Infantry, "The Old Guard," re- enact the story of the American presidency from its early days to the present.

The colorful production took the audience from the Constitu- tional Congress through the space age and the Vietnam conflict.

Thursday, January 19, 1989

On the following morning, 9,000 high school students gath- ered at the Washington National Guard Armory to hear both the president-elect and vice presi- dent-elect discuss the importance of education to America's future and the future of American students.

A little later, at the John F. Kennedy Center for the Perform- ing Arts, 6,000 fans of the first lady gathered in all three of the center's major theaters to pay tribute to her.

Mrs. Bush, who was introduced by Marilyn Quayle, in turn intro- duced her daughter and daughters- in-law to the audience and, with obvious pride, announced, "All my children, incidentally, married way above themselves."

Performers at the Salute to the First Lady included the Houston Symphony, the Preservation Hall Jazz Band, The Gatlin Brothers, and the Mora Arriagas Mariachi Band—with the Bushes' 11-year- old granddaughter Noelle per- forming on the accordion and tambourine.

And in the afternoon, 13,000 well-wishers crowded the Nation- al Museum of American History to enjoy a few refreshments with the vice president-elect at the Vice Presidential Reception. The line of guests stretched down Constitution Avenue to 14th Street, around the museum and back almost to the starting point on Constitution Avenue.

The Inaugural Gala that evening featured an outstanding cast in- cluding: dancers Gregg Burge, Hinton Battle and Tommy Tune; singers Roberta Peters, Loretta Lynn, Crystal Gayle, the Oak Ridge Boys, Nell Carter and Frank Sinatra; cellist Yo Yo Ma; and actor Michael Crawford, who recreated a scene from his hit Broadway musical, "Phantom of the Opera." The event was telecast nationally on CBS.

Of the more than 240 Bush relatives who came to town for the inauguration, 22 members of the immediate family stayed at

The crowd gathers to witness the inauguration of the 41st President of the United States.

Navy midshipmen supervise the final preparations for the inaugural ceremonies.

Blair House, the historic official guest residence located directly across Pennsylvania Avenue from the White House.

Blair House, where Virginian Robert E. Lee turned down the job of commanding the Union forces before the Civil War, is today used as a guest house for visiting dignitaries and heads of state. The newly renovated home was suitably "inaugurated" by the entire Bush family who stayed there before the ceremonies.

George Walker Bush, the president-elect's son, later described the scene, as the Blair House staff tended to the needs of the family "surrounded by about 10 screaming grandkids that I think brought the whole scene down to earth. There were toys, tractors out on the patio, people riding those little three-wheelers, and, all in all, it was a great scene."

In the midst of the bedlam, Bush recounted to ABC News'

Peter Jennings, the soon-to-be first lady played a game of Simon Says with her exuberant grandchildren, "and she lost."

Inauguration Day, January 20, 1989

There are events that people want to be a part of, no matter how small their part may be. An inauguration of a president is one of those events.

It was not surprising, then, that people who did not have tickets to the swearing-in ceremony arrived early to stake their claims on the nearest available turf and to hold their positions against all comers. By the time the sun rose on Friday morning, the spectators were already well-entrenched, with their blankets, containers of coffee, and personal stereo receivers.

Some came to hear the new president's message for the country. Others came to bear a message to him. Some carried signs and posters; others wore them.

They were, perhaps, more demonstrative than the center of attention, the president-elect.

"He's remarkably calm," son George told ABC News on the morning of the inauguration. "I saw him at breakfast in his pajamas—the same pajamas he wore about two years ago, I think. I saw him at church, and he's ready to take the oath of office and ready to be the president. I didn't find any anxiety in him or

any unnecessary tension.

"He's a quiet man, and he doesn't get very emotional about things."

As the Congressional Chorus sang "Shenandoah," the crowds waited at the Capitol for President and Mrs. Reagan and President-elect and Mrs. Bush to leave the White House for the Capitol.

The limousines dispatched by Congress arrived at the White House, and President-elect Bush and President Reagan, who had been having coffee together in the Blue Room, left together for Capitol Hill with their congressional escorts. The limousine bearing Bush and Reagan displayed inaugural license plates reading: "USA 1."

The congressional escorts included the leadership of both houses of the legislature and of both major political parties. For the duration of this day, and this event, political adversaries such as the Rev. Jesse Jackson and the Rev. Jerry Falwell could join together in civility—and even friendship. Coretta Scott King, widow of slain civil rights leader Martin Luther King, Jr., joined the guests for the swearing-in ceremony.

In keeping with the bicentennial theme of the inauguration, the president-elect took the oath of office with the Bible used 200 years before by George Washington, as well as his own family Bible.

In his inaugural address, the new president spoke of a "new

"reeze" blowing in the nation and he world. He urged the nation to each out to "those who cannot ree themselves of enslavement to hatever addiction—drugs, welare, demoralization that rules the lums.

"A nation refreshed by freedom tands ready to push on," the resident said. "There is new round to be broken and new ction to be taken.

"I see history as a book with nany pages," he said. "Today a hapter begins: a small and stately tory of unity, diversity and enerosity, shared, and written, ogether."

After the swearing-in, before he new president and his party oined Congressional leaders for unch in the Capitol's Statuary Iall, former President and Mrs. eagan walked to a waiting helipter, which took them for one nal lap around the Capitol and hen whisked them to Andrews ir Force Base. There, they boarded a jet aircraft that took them ome to California.

On the way back to California, he former president talked about is successor with *The Washington ost* reporter Lou Cannon. "He Bush) was the one I would rather e there than anyone else," eagan said.

"Beyond a doubt, the Reagans re sentimental people," Cannon rote later. "I suspect that we will uiss them, no matter what we ink of them. I suspect that they ill miss us, too."

Meanwhile, the new president

was telling other guests at the congressional luncheon that the new title was taking a little getting used to. After the ceremony, as Mr. Reagan was leaving, the sergeant-at-arms said, "Mr. President," and Bush, thinking the call was directed at Mr. Reagan, did not budge.

It took a reminder from the new first lady—"something between an affectionate hug and a kidney punch"—to bring him back to reality, President Bush said, to appreciative laughter from everyone, including Mrs. Bush.

The president and vice president were presented Lenox crystal bowls, hand-etched with the Capitol on one side and a grove of cherry trees on the other. They were, said Sen. Wendell Ford (D-Ken.), gifts from the Congress and the American people. Rep. Robert Michel (R-Ill.), the House minority leader, gave the president a plaque on which had been mounted the letter opener used to open the envelopes containing the electoral votes that had made Bush president. Michel also presented the president with a portrait of Martin Van Buren, the only prior sitting vice president to be elected president in his own right.

Concurrently, the state governors gathered in the historic Cash Room at the Treasury Department, the first time that inaugural festivities have been held there since 1869. Hosted by Chief of Staff John Sununu, the

governors celebrated the beginning of another century of peace, prosperity and independence.

The parade was late getting under way. The cars had barely left "the Hill" when, to the delight of the crowds (and the consternation of the Secret Service), President and Mrs. Bush got out of the presidential limousine and strolled down Pennsylvania Avenue, waving to spectators. It was an action they would repeat several times—alternately riding and walking—all along the parade route. Vice President and Mrs. Quayle followed suit. At one point, Mrs. Bush got out of the car and jogged to the sidelines to plant a kiss on NBC weather announcer Willard Scott, who had hosted the opening celebration two days earlier.

The parade was a gargantuan affair led by Grand Marshals Bob Hope and Chuck Yeager, with more than 75 floats, 211 parade units, a 40-foot helium Popeye balloon and about 12,000 participants. Among the marching units were the Kennebunk (Maine) High School Marching Band and the Yale University Concert Band, from the new president's alma mater, an ensemble that had to schedule emergency rehearsals to practice the art of walking and playing simultaneously.

Along the parade route, spectators were visibly surprised—and pleased—to hear the voice of Vice President Quayle emanating from the vice presidential limousine. "Hello, there," the vice president

said, and the crowds waved vigorously in response. The vice president had discovered the car's public address capabilities and was putting them to effective use.

On their arrival at the White House, the Bushes and Quayles joined their families in the review stand to watch the rest of the parade pass by. The Quayle children "covered" the activities by taking photographs to be included in this book.

Inaugural Ball

No inaugural event is as entrenched in the inaugural tradition as the Inaugural Ball. This year there were 11 balls in 10 separate locations: The John F. Kennedy Center for the Performing Arts, Union Station, the Pension Building, the National Air and Space Museum, the Washington Hilton Hotel, the Omni Shoreham Hotel, the Sheraton Washington Hotel, the Washington National Guard Armory, the J. W. Marriott Hotel and two balls at the Washington Convention Center.

The presidential and vice presidential parties, in the course of paying a call at each site, crossed paths at the J. W. Marriott, site of the second Young Americans Ball. "We were in the building and heard a little noise and wanted to come see what it was all about," Vice President Quayle jokingly told the ballgoers.

Shortly before 11 p.m. President

and Mrs. Bush arrived at the National Air and Space Museum, where the Texas and South Carolina delegations were in mid-celebration. The Bushes danced one dance, and then Bill Harrington's orchestra swung quickly into "Deep in the Heart o Texas." The response from the floor was deafening.

Saturday, January 21, 1989

The following morning, the new president and his family participated in an event unusual in modern presidential history: an open house at the White House. More than 4,000 people were welcomed onto the South Lawn during the three-hour event. Some had waited in line for nearly 12 hours for the opportunity to see and perhaps shake hands with the new chief executive.

There were no special arrange ments; admission was on a first-come, first-served basis.

In an upstairs window, Marsha Bush, one of the youngest of the 10 Bush grandchildren, peered out at the waiting crowds in delight and amazement. The crowd was no less amazing to veteran Washingtonians.

Two events unique to this inaugural occurred on Saturday, both at Constitution Hall. The first was "George to George—20(Years," a pageant for children, which brought the history of the presidency to the young audienc from their own viewpoint. Narra-

Pension Building

tor Wilford Brimley was joined by special guests Big Bird and Maria from the popular "Sesame Street" program.

The pageant took the children through American history from the first president to the latest and ended with an impromptu re-creation of an inaugural parade, which involved the audience and the entire auditorium.

In the evening, "Mission Impossible" star Greg Morris narrated an original combination of song and commentary, "I Am an American," to set the tone for festivities during "An American Salute to Democracy." Actor Wilford Brimley recited the history of one of our best-loved songs of hope and patriotism, "The Battle Hymn of the Republic," followed by an inspiring speech by Vice President Quayle. The celebration was capped by House Minority Leader Robert H. Michel (R-Ill.)

performing a stirring rendition of "God Bless America." Then, the Quayle family returned to the stage to join him, the entire audience, the Mormon Tabernacle Choir, the U.S. Air Force Band and the Singing Sergeants in a second chorus of this favorite song.

When singer-songwriter James Taylor once sang that "rock 'n' roll is music, now," he meant that the nation's musical palate had become accustomed to a broader range of tastes than had been true in the past. If further evidence were needed, the "Celebration for Young Americans" provided it.

On Saturday evening, thousands of rhythm and blues fans packed the Washington Convention Center to see and hear a group of legendary performers who helped to break down the barriers that had formerly separated white music from black

music.

For those who loved the music, the lineup of performers was like a dream come true. It included Billy Preston, Percy Sledge, Willie Dixon, Jimmie and Stevie Ray Vaughan, Dr. John, Sam Moore, Eddie Floyd, Bo Diddley, Delbert McClinton—and isn't that the new chairman of the Republican National Committee, Lee Atwater, up there jamming with Sam Moore to the tune of "Hi-Heeled Sneakers?"

Yes, it was, as a matter of fact with the new president of the United States alongside him, gamely strumming his new guitar emblazoned with the words "The Prez." The guitar was an on-stage gift from Atwater.

"Without question," said the president, "this is the most active event of this inauguration."

Sunday, January 22, 1989

The events of inaugural week came to a close with a National Prayer Service of Thanksgiving at the Washington Cathedral. The cathedral, begun in 1907, has been under construction ever since, and completion is not anticipated until sometime in the 1990s. But it remains an awe-inspiring sight, a contemporary architectural achievement based on the best models of the past—and in continual development—rather like the nation itself.

It was sung at the Inaugural Gala rather than at the prayer service, but the words to the official song of the Bicentennial of the U.S. Constitution may well have come to mind to members of the congregation that Sunday morning:

So Many Voices Sing America's Song
Lyrics by Bruce Belland
Music by Robert F. Brunner

We come from everywhere...
  we're called Americans
From every distant shore,
  but what matters more
  ...is we're Americans.
United by the promise etched
  beneath the flame
That says beyond this golden
  door you enter
  ...everyone's the same.

So many voices sing America's
  song
So many dreamers come from
  different shores
  to proudly sing along,
So many colors in our rainbow
  choir
So many hearts from many
  homelands all with one desire,
To raise their voices in a country
  that's free,
To blend their music with
  America's, from sea to shining
  sea,

So many voices from so many
  lands
Make one great song when we
  join voices
  ...hearts
  ...and hands.

Clyde Linsley is a Virginia-based writer.

■
The Mormon Tabernacle Choir.

◨
An oversized American flag decorated the parade route.

Inaugural
Opening
Celebration

◼

A demonstration by the
U.S. Navy's 21 fighter
planes.

■
The honored guests
arrive for the Opening
Celebration.

■
Over 40,000 spectators
gathered for the after-
noon's entertainment.

■
The Vice President-elect,
the President-elect and
their families watch the
opening festivities from
their viewing stand.

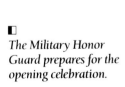
The Military Honor
Guard prepares for the
opening celebration.

One of the Golden
Knights of the U.S.
Army drops in on the
festivities.

Up With People added
a lively note to the
activities.

■
George Bush lights the ceremonial flame and invites the audience to turn on their thousand points of light.

■
The Opening Celebration fireworks begin.

The American
Presidential Pageant

Important moments of our history were re-enacted during the American Presidential Pageant at Constitution Hall.

Inaugural Dinners

■
Recently restored Union Station was one of the three sites for the Inaugural Dinners.

■
The Bushes and the Quayles acknowledge Co-chairman Bobby Holt and his wife Joanie at the Union Station dinner.

■
Co-chairman Penne Korth addresses the guests at the Corcoran Gallery dinner.

■
The guests are entertained by the Strolling Strings at the Corcoran Gallery as they arrive for dinner.

■
The President-elect greets friends from Texas at the Union Station Dinner.

The Pension Building.

The president's son George responds to questions from the press corps.

The President-elect visits with guests at the Inaugural Dinner at the Corcoran Gallery.

Looking Forward: An Inaugural Forum

■
*Peter Vidmar, 1984
Olympic Gold Medalist
at the Forum.*

■
*The Eastern High
School Choir entertains
the attendees at the
Forum.*

■
*The DC National Guard
Armory was the perfect
setting for "Looking
Forward: An Inaugural
Forum."*

■
*The President-elect,
accompanied by
Congresswoman Lynn
Martin (R-Ill.), speaks
to award winning
students and their
teachers during the
Forum.*

Salute to the First Lady

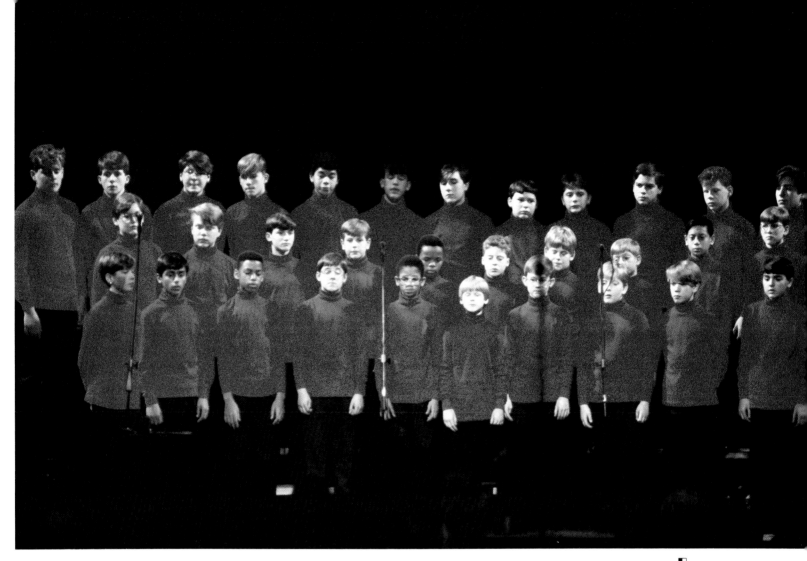

■
Mrs. Bush introduces
her distinguished ladies.

▫
Mrs. Bush at the
Inaugural Dinner.

▫
Barbara Bush greets
familiar faces as she
walks down the aisle of
the Kennedy Center.

■
American Boys Choir.

▫
Noelle Bush performed
with the Mora Arriagas
Mariachi Band.

The Vice President's Reception

■
Dan Quayle enjoys spending a few moments talking with his guests.

◨
Vice President-elect Dan Quayle, seen here with his wife and parents, greets Inaugural guests at the Museum of American History.

◻
The honor guard at the Vice Presidential Reception.

The
Inaugural Gala

The Quayles and the Bushes on the stage with the Mormon Tabernacle Choir during the finale of the Inaugural Gala.

American Ballet Theater's principal ballerina, Susan Jaffe, performs the dance of The Dying Swan.

■
Tommy Tune sings and dances from one of his Broadway hits.

▣
Kentucky Country and the Idaho Jr. Jammer Fiddlers charm the gala audience.

■
Nell Carter performs with her troupe during the Inaugural Gala.

■
Michael Crawford re-creates a scene from Broadway's "Phantom of the Opera."

■
George Bush shares a moment with his grand-daughter Jenna during the Gala.

Friday, January 20, 1989

■
*A moment of reflection
started the day.*

■
*The Capitol grounds
before the public begins
to arrive.*

■
*On Inaugural morning,
the Capitol stands ready
for another change of
command.*

■
*The National Mall
teems with excitement.*

◩
*The view from the
Capitol overlooking the
inaugural platform.*

▣
*Members of the United
States Senate observe
the orderly transfer of
power.*

Inaugural Address of the President

The U.S. Capitol

12:05 p.m. EST

January 20, 1989

Mr. Chief Justice, Mr. President, Vice President Quayle, Senator Mitchell, Speaker Wright, Senator Dole, Congressman Michel, and fellow citizens, neighbors and friends.

There is a man here who has earned a lasting place in our hearts and in our history. President Reagan, on behalf of our nation, I thank you for the wonderful things that you have done for America.

I've just repeated word-for-word the oath taken by George Washington 200 years ago; and the Bible on which I placed my hand is the Bible on which he placed his.

It is right that the memory of Washington be with us today, not only because this is our bicentennial Inauguration, but because Washington remains the father of our country. And he would, I think, be gladdened by this day. For today is the concrete expression of a stunning fact: Our continuity these 200 years since our government began.

We meet on democracy's front porch. A good place to talk as neighbors, and as friends. For this is a day when our nation is made whole, when our differences, for a moment, are suspended.

And my first act as President is a prayer. I ask you to bow your heads.

Heavenly Father, we bow our heads and thank you for your love. Accept our thanks for the peace that yields this day and the shared faith that makes its continuance likely. Make us strong to do your work, willing to heed and hear your will, and write on our hearts these words: "Use power to help people." For we are given power not to advance our own purposes, nor to make a great show in the world, nor a name. There is but one just use of power, and it is to serve people. Help us to remember, Lord. Amen.

I come before you and assume the presidency at a moment rich with promise. We live in a peaceful, prosperous time, but we can make it better.

For a new breeze is blowing, and a world refreshed by freedom seems reborn; for in man's heart, if not in fact, the day of the dictator is over. The totalitarian era is passing, its old ideas blown away like leaves from an ancient lifeless tree.

A new breeze is blowing, and a nation refreshed by freedom stands ready to push on. There is new ground to be broken, and new action to be taken.

There are times when the future seems thick as a fog; you sit and wait, hoping the mists will lift and reveal the right path.

But this is a time when the future seems a door you can walk right through—into a room called Tomorrow.

Great nations of the world are moving toward democracy—through the door to freedom.

Men and women of the world move toward free markets—through the door to prosperity.

The people of the world agitate for free expression and free

thought—through the door to the moral and intellectual satisfactions that only liberty allows.

We know what works: Freedom works. We know what's right: Freedom is right. We know how to secure a more just and prosperous life for man on Earth: through free markets, free speech, free elections, and the exercise of free will unhampered by the state.

For the first time in this century—for the first time in perhaps all history—man does not have to invent a system by which to live. We don't have to talk late into the night about which form of government is better. We don't have to wrest justice from the kings. We only have to summon it from within ourselves.

We must act on what we know. I take as my guide the hope of a saint: In crucial things, unity—in important things, diversity—in all things, generosity.

America today is a proud, free nation, decent and civil—a place we cannot help but love. We know in our hearts, not loudly and proudly, but as a simple fact, that this country has meaning beyond what we see, and that our strength is a force for good.

But have we changed as a nation even in our time? Are we enthralled with material things, less appreciative of the nobility of work and sacrifice?

My friends, we are not the sum of our possessions. They are not the measure of our lives. In our hearts we know what matters. We cannot hope only to leave our children a bigger car, a bigger bank account. We must hope to give them a sense of what it means to be a loyal friend, a loving parent, a citizen who leaves his home, his neighborhood and town better than he found it.

And what do we want the men and women who work with us to say when we are no longer there? That we were more driven to suc-

ceed than anyone around us? Or that we stopped to ask if a sick child had gotten better, and stayed a moment there to trade a word of friendship?

No president, no government, can teach us to remember what is best in what we are. But if a man you have chosen to lead this government can help make a difference; if he can celebrate the quieter, deeper successes that are made not of gold and silk, but of better hearts and finer souls; if he can do these things, then he must.

America is never wholly herself unless she is engaged in high moral principle. We as a people have such a purpose today. It is to make kinder the face of the nation and gentler the face of the world.

My friends, we have work to do. There are the homeless, lost and roaming, there are the children who have nothing—no love and no normalcy—there are those who cannot free themselves of enslavement to whatever addiction—drugs, welfare, the demoralization that rules the slums. There is crime to be conquered, the rough crime of the streets. There are young women to be helped who are about to become mothers of children they can't care for and might not love. They need our care, our guidance, and our education though we bless them for choosing life.

The old solution, the old way, was to think that public money alone could end these problems. But we have learned that that is not so. And in any case, our funds are low. We have a deficit to bring down. We have more will than wallet, but will is what we need.

We will make the hard choices, looking at what we have and perhaps allocating it differently, making our decisions based on honest need and prudent safety.

And then we will do the wisest thing of all—we will turn to the only resource we have that in times of need always grows: the goodness and the courage of the American people.

And I am speaking of a new engagement in the lives of others —a new activism, hands-on, and involved, that gets the job done. We must bring in the generations, harnessing the unused talent of the elderly and the unfocused energy of the young. For not only leadership is passed from generation to generation, but so is stewardship. And the generation born after the Second World War has come of age.

I have spoken of a thousand points of light—of all the community organizations that are spread like stars throughout the nation, doing good.

We will work hand in hand, encouraging, sometimes leading, sometimes being led, rewarding. We will work on this in the White House, in the Cabinet agencies. I will go to the people and the programs that are the brighter points of light, and I'll ask every member of my government to become involved.

The old ideas are new again because they are not old, they are timeless: duty, sacrifice, commitment, and a patriotism that finds its expression in taking part and pitching in.

We need a new engagement, too, between the Executive and the Congress. The challenges before us will be thrashed out with the House and the Senate. And we must ensure that America stands before the world united— strong, at peace and fiscally sound. But, of course, things may be difficult.

We need compromise; we've had dissension. We need harmony; we've had a chorus of discordant voices.

For Congress, too, has changed in our time. There has grown a certain divisiveness. We have seen the hard looks and heard the statements in which not each other's ideas are challenged, but each other's motives. And our great parties have too often been far apart and untrusting of each other.

It's been this way since Vietnam. That war cleaves us still. But, friends, that war began in earnest a quarter of a century ago, and surely the statute of limitations has been reached. This is a fact: The final lesson of Vietnam is that no great nation can long afford to be sundered by a memory.

A new breeze is blowing—and the old bipartisanship must be made new again.

To my friends—and, yes, I do mean friends—in the loyal opposition—and, yes, I mean loyal, I put out my hand.

I am putting out my hand to you, Mr. Speaker.

I am putting out my hand to you, Mr. Majority Leader.

For this is the thing: This is the age of the offered hand.

And we can't turn back clocks and I don't want to. But when our fathers were young, Mr. Speaker, our differences ended at the water's edge. And we don't wish to turn back time, but when our mothers were young, Mr. Majority Leader, the Congress and the Executive were capable of working together to produce a budget on which this nation would live. Let us negotiate soon, and hard. But in the end, let us produce.

The American people await action. They didn't send us here to bicker. They ask us to rise above the merely partisan. "In crucial things, unity"—and this, my friends, is crucial.

To the world, too, we offer new engagement and a renewed vow; we will stay strong to protect the peace. The "offered hand" is a reluctant fist, once made, strong and can be used with great effect.

There are today Americans who are held against their will in for-

eign lands and Americans who are unaccounted for. Assistance can be shown here and will be long remembered. Goodwill begets goodwill. Good faith can be a spiral that endlessly moves on.

Great nations like great men must keep their word. When America says something, America means it, whether a treaty, or an agreement, or a vow made on marble steps. We will always try to speak clearly, for candor is a compliment. But subtlety, too, is good and has its place.

While keeping our alliances and friendships around the world strong, ever strong, we will continue the new closeness with the Soviet Union, consistent both with our security and with progress. One might say that our new relationship in part reflects the triumph of hope and strength over experience. But hope is good. And so is strength. And vigilance.

Here today are tens of thousands of our citizens who feel the understandable satisfaction of those who have taken part in democracy and seen their hopes fulfilled.

But my thoughts have been turning the past few days to those who would be watching at home.

To an older fellow who will throw a salute by himself when the flag goes by, and the woman who will tell her sons the words of the battle hymns. I don't mean this to be sentimental. I mean that on days like this, we remember that we are all part of a continuum, inescapably connected by the ties that bind.

Our children are watching in schools throughout our great land. And to them I say, thank you for watching democracy's big day. For democracy belongs to us

all, and freedom is like a beautiful kite that can go higher and higher with the breeze.

And to all I say, no matter what your circumstances or where you are, you are part of this day; you are part of the life of our great nation.

A president is neither prince nor pope, and I don't seek "a window on men's souls." In fact, I yearn for a greater tolerance, an easy-goingness about each other's attitudes and way of life.

There are a few clear areas in which we as a society must rise up united and express our intolerance. The most obvious now is drugs. And when that first cocaine was smuggled in on a ship, it may as well have been a deadly bacteria, so much has it hurt the body, the soul of our country. And there is much to be done and to be said, but take my word for it—this scourge will stop.

And so there is much to do; and tomorrow the work begins.

And I do not mistrust the future; I do not fear what is ahead. For our problems are large, but our heart is larger. Our challenges are great, but our will is greater. And if our flaws are endless, God's love is truly boundless.

Some see leadership as high drama and the sound of trumpets calling. And sometimes it is that. But I see history as a book with many pages—and each day we fill a page with acts of hopefulness and meaning.

The new breeze blows, a page turns, the story unfolds—and so today a chapter begins—a small and stately story of unity, diversity and generosity—shared, written, together.

Thank you. God bless you. And God bless the United States of America.

▪
Ambassadors representing their countries here in the United States were among the distinguished guests.

▪
Mrs. Coretta Scott King joined the many inaugural guests.

▪
Members of the working press record the event for posterity.

■
*The Chiefs of the
Armed Forces were
represented on the
platform as well.*

■
*The President and First
Lady acknowledge the
thundering applause.*

□
*The President with his
mother after the
Inaugural Address.*

■
President Bush advocates service as part of the "new breeze" blowing across the land.

■
The Bush family shows their approval after their father is sworn in as president.

The Bushes frequently
left their car to walk and
greet spectators along
the parade route.

The Bushes and the
Quayles joined their
families in the reviewing
stands to watch the
parade.

Spectators anxiously
await the first glimpse
of the President.

The University of Texas
Marching Band.

109

The 1989 Inaugural Parade

■
An "Avenger" aircraft like the one President Bush piloted during World War II and members of his squadron are featured on this float.

■
Members of the family stay occupied during the parade festivities.

The Inaugural Balls

The Bushes greet the ball goers at the Omni Shoreham.

The Texans and South Carolinians celebrated at the Air and Space Museum.

The United States Herald Trumpets announce the entrance of the President and Vice President.

The President and the
First Lady dance their
first dance of the
evening at the Pension
Building.

Mr. and Mrs. Holt and
Mr. and Mrs. Korth
enjoy the crowd at the
Inaugural Ball.

The Vice President and
Mrs. Quayle waltz at
the Union Station Ball.

The Quayles make their
entrance at the Union
Station Ball.

Revelry at the Inaugural
Ball at Union Station.

Saturday, January 21, 1989

White House American Welcome

■
George Bush spends a few moments after the open house on Saturday with his grandchildren on the lawn of the White House.

■
President and Mrs. Bush show Americans their new home during the White House American Welcome.

◪
During the historic open house, more than 4,000 Americans were welcomed to tour the official rooms and grounds of the White House.

"George to George—200 Years"
A Children's Inaugural Festival

Mrs. Bush meets Big Bird with her grand- children.

Flags of all kinds added to the pageantry of the George to George celebration.

Children of all ages celebrated at the George to George celebration event at Constitution Hall.

Celebration
For Young
Americans

■
The Celebration for Young Americans was considered by the President to be "the most active inaugural event."

■
Bo Diddley and Ron Wood entertain at the Celebration for Young Americans.

■
President Bush "jams" with Lee Atwater during the youth celebration.

■
Clutching the "Prez" guitar, a gift from Lee Atwater, President Bush waves to the animated crowd.

An American Tribute to Democracy

■
The Quayle family joins House Minority Leader Robert H. Michel in singing "God Bless America."

◰
The Mormon Tabernacle Choir, the U.S. Air Force Band and the Singing Sergeants entertain the vice president's family and guests during the American Salute to Democracy.

National Prayer Service of Thanksgiving

The Bushes and Quayles join the rest of America in a National Prayer Service of Thanksgiving at the Washington Cathedral.

The Inauguration of a President is a national celebration. Its success could not be possible without the cooperation and dedication of numerous companies and organizations, the men and women of the nation's Armed Forces, and, of course, the unwavering inaugural staff. Their spirit, enthusiasm and many contributions were instrumental to the sense of excitement with which we start this third century of the American Presidency. We are extremely grateful for their dedicated service and continued good will.

The American Bicentennial Presidential Inaugural Committee

Co-Chairmen
Bobby Holt
Penne Percy Korth

Executive Director
Stephen M. Studdert

Special Advisor to the Inaugural Committee
Ronald C. Kaufman

Finance Chairman
Walter J. Ganzi, Jr.

Finance Co-Chairmen
Mel Sembler
Joseph Zappala

Operations
William D. Harris, *Principal Deputy to the Executive Director and Director of Operations*
Michael V. Miller, *Senior Deputy Director*
Benjamin R. Turner, *Assistant Deputy Director*
James H. Baker, *Director*
Linda Long, *Director*
Frank Thornwald, *Director*
C. Blake Williams, *Director*
Chuck Williams, *Director*
F.C. Duke Zeller, *Director*
Philip J. Anderson
Stanley Antrim
Ian Barrie
Suzanne Bertain
Marc Bien
Allison Bloch
Charles (Sandy) Blunt
Leo Brady
Steven E. Carruthers
Barbara Cebuhar
Suzanne Chase
Kimberly Ciresa
Roy Coffee
Jon Coley
Dianne DeRoze
Dorothy Deas
Tracy Doherty
Michael Donlon
Alicia Dugan
Jerry Eatherly
R. Scott Engelson
Greg Farris
D. Hollis (Chip) Felkel
Michael Fones
John Ford
Timothy Galbraith
Ashton Graham
Sarah Harton
Mark Hatfield
Margaret Hazelrigg
Bill Johnson
Kenneth Kearns
Judy Kornfeld
Hendricks Lindsey
Michael Luckey
Anne Marbach
Karen Martinez
Ferdinand McGinn
Jennifer Mills
Jane Moore
Noel Anne Murphy
Elizabeth G. Nichols
Timothy Patrick O'Neill
Elizabeth F. Ollison
Thomas Panuzio
Vernon Parker
Craig Pattee

Julie Perrier
Christine Peterson
Nancy Pilon
Frederick Pouring
Mary Elizabeth Quint
Donald E. Rauner
Thomas Scott
John Tenuta
E. Jane Turner
Dolores Weiss
Carlisle Williams

Administration
Donald A. Clarey, *Director*
Kathy Armstrong, *Deputy Director*
David Balfour, *Group Director*
Susan Loud, *Group Director*
Thomas C. McCully, *Group Director*
Linda Reed O'Meara, *Group Director*
B.J. Rogers, *Group Director*
Alison Shurtleff, *Group Director*
Jaqueline Smith, *Group Director*
Kelsey Marshall, *Disability Advisor*

Emily Aertker
Zach Allen
Mary Anderson
Richard Boase
Philip Brennan
Robert Brooks
Philip Coolidge Brooks, Jr.
Robert D. Brown
Douglas Cameron
Anthony Campos
Bobby Carr
Jimee Youngchul Choi
Peter Christian
Lilia Clemons
David Andrew Crowder
Joanne (Jaye) Darby
William Daroff
David Dawson
Susan Dawson
Lee Dickey
Thomas Doyle
Marguerite Duffy
Thomas Elio Duplessie
Charlotte Ellis
Michael Evans
Michelle Federico
Judy Fisher
William S. Fleishell
Robert Gleason, Jr.
Lisa A. Gorove
Ralf Greenwood
Ana Maria Guevara
John Hannigan
Robert W. Harkins
David Hart
Audrey Hendricks
Sarah Hendrickson
Aphrodite Hero
William Hervey
Dwight Holloway
Gary Michael Huggins
Ruth Mayree Jeffers
Daniel Jerore
Elton Johnson, Jr.
S. Russell Jones
Edgar H. Jowett, III
William H. Jun
Susannah Kent
Cheryl Kienel
John Knechtle
Afsoun Kuhnsman
Iva Marie LaFauvier
Charles Leach, III
Cybele Lee
Patricia Limbacher
Suzanne List
Ellen MacNair

Sarah Madden
Patricia Mathews
Patricia McCloskey
Michael McKenna
Paul McNeill
Paula Meltzer
Patricia Militzer
Terry Mitchell
Adelaida Artime Morley
Adeeb Neam
Patricia Nolan
Virginia Oldham
Nicholas Panuzio
Gina Piacentini
Lewis Pipkin
James Pitts
Melissa Poulton
David Puglia
Carolina Regan
Eric Rehmann
Steve R. Richards
Mildred Ross
Stephen Schwartz
Elly Seng
Ernest Silva
Stephen Slipek
James St. John
Bette R. Sterkx
Scott Styles
Nancye Schumann Sweet
Carol Thompson
Timothy Unes
Tiffany Van der Stokker
W. Rock Vaughan
James Stuart Victor, III
Julie Wadler
Tracey Warren
Robert Washington
William Whitlock
Thomas Yedinak
Courtney Zwart

Communications
Laurie Snow Turner, *Director*
Susan Fertig-Dykes, *Group Director*
C.J. (Jim) Moore, *Group Director*
Betsy White, *Group Director*
Ed Cassidy, *Spokesman for the Co-Chairmen*
Claire Austin
Claudia Barlow
Janet Barnes (Staihar)
Peter Borromeo
Stuart (Brewser) Brown
Mary Mein (Mimi) Carter
Lawrence Cirignano
Teresa Clark
Joyce Blair Curry
John Herr
Holly Hopkins
Gregory Hopkins
William Laahs
Sherri Marsh
Daniel McLagon
David Rogers
Victoria Scully
Stan Smith
Mary Owen Smolko
Tracy Spahr

Congressional Relations
Craig R. Helsing, *Director*
William D. Fritts, *Group Director*
Paul L. Powell, *Group Director*
Tim Hecht
Megan E. Molloy
Shiree Sanchez
Debra Westra

Executive Office
Betsy Ekonomou, *Deputy to the Chairman*
John A. Kelly, *Executive Assistant*

Deborah McMahon, *Deputy to the Chairman*
Skip Abernathy
Peggy Abrahamson
Traci Aultman
Andrew Ballard
Barbara Bauman
Claudio Benedi
David M. Carney
Lee Carter
Paul J. Collins, Jr.
Demetrios Coupounas
Kate Flaherty
Matthew Frank
Kimberly A. Healy
Susan Hogan
Jeffrey Hunter
Rebekah Johnson
Jacqueline A. Kennedy
Perry Liles
Leo W. Nadeau
Frederick Nutt
Fred Sainz
Barbara Schlech
Garlef (Carl) Schlieker
Janet Schuler
Jacklyn Sunderland
Pam Thompson
Sheryl Vanniere
Catherine E. Wood

Finance
Lynn Collins Urbanski, *Director*
Jeanne Johnson, *Deputy Director*

Fundraising
Walter J. Ganzi, Jr., *Director*
Sandra Baxter
Teresa Bieker
H. Spofford Canfield, IV
Ann Herberger
Jeanne Johnson
Christopher Kidder
Mary McGinnis
Kelly Schaben
James Sears
Mel Sembler
Lynn Urbanski
Mary Pat Wilson
Joe Zappala

Gala
Joseph W. Canzeri, *Director*
Douglas Baker
Terry L. Baxter
Margaret Glasscock
Ronald Hamway
Mark Henson
Gaylynn Hooley
Sherri J. McVay
James Meszaros
Sean O'Malley
Janine A. Stanhope

General Counsel
Jan W. Baran, *General Counsel*
Trevor Potter, *Deputy General Counsel*
Walter Barbee
Roberta Barbee
Courtney (Juan) Cunningham
Carl Frank
Kemp Robert Harshman
Jeffrey Holik
David Ladd
Jeanne Lawrence
Nancy Lee
Lee Levine
Michael Newman
F. Richard Pappas
Gant Redmon
Gerald Sherman

Bruce Soll
Lynn West

General Services Administration
James D. Arthur, *Coordinator*

Invitations
Gordon C. James, *Director*
Christy Cobb, *Deputy Director*
Beth E. Griffin, *Deputy Director*
Rebecca Honeycutt, *Deputy Director*
Anne Slichter, *Deputy Director*
Timothy Bartlett
Gregory Beam
Robert Berry
Amy Louisa Buckley
Mike Connell
Dawn DeVoe
James S. Dineen, Jr.
Dwayne Gathers
Tamra Hissom
Anita Jones
Rebecca Nelson
Eva Neterowicz
Michael O'Connell
Kari Patten
Victoria Pittman-Waller
Catherine Ramsey
Anita Sweeney
Joseph Taylor

Marketing
Grant R. Curtis, *Director*
Douglas E. Ryder, *Deputy Director*
Joesph Bailey
Marjan Bianca Bavand
Christopher Beavers
Jeffrey Bengtson
Timothy G. Bobbitt
Laura Breyer
Donald Burley
Jane Carpenter
P. Roberts Coffin
Jill Collins
Cheryl L. Crispen
Noel Dawson
Lee Anne Elliot
Alexander Gilchrist
Lisa Goddard
Karen Gossett
John Gullickson
Karen Harbert
Leslie Charlene Hare
Kym Hill
Bernard Hite
Evan Hughes
James Hunter
George Johnson
Ryne L. Johnson
Barry Jordan
John Lane
Scott Lansell
Margaret R. Mankin
Claire C. Martin
Marisa McCarthy
Farrell P. McHugh
Barbara McLeod
George Mentz
Palmer Murray
William E. Quinby
John Roberts
Doug Ryder
Thomas Saidy
Linda Schatz
Maggie Scott
John R. Shrewder, Jr.
Stacey Silva
Nancy Smith
Douglas (Bemis) Smith
Charles Stanley
Jocelyn Stevenson
Tim Thompson
Michael 'Dane' Waters
John Richard Watson
Lanny Wiles
Neal Wise
Bonnie Wolfe
Teddy Wu
Howard 'Skip' Yeager
S. Edward Young

Public Liaison
Helen R. Cameron, *Director*
Ellen Conaway, *Deputy Director*
Karen Castleman, *Group Director*

Norman Cummings, *Group Director*
Bruce Holmberg, *Group Director*
Colleen Padden, *Group Director*
Linda White, *Group Director*
Allison Adams
Clifford Alderman
Lenora Alexander
Andrew Armstrong
Cynthia Ayers
Andrea Balletta
Henry Barbour
Charles Blackburn
David C. Blee
E. Perry Bolger, Jr.
Patrick R. Booher, Jr.
Raymond Briscuso, Jr.
Kay Bruce
Leigh Ann Buller
Christopher Burnham
Robert Carter
Lauren Childress
Mary Ann Christensen
Alice Cockerham
Christina Collins
Melinda Cox
William Dalcol
Roberto G. De Posada
Veronica DeNardo
Michael Dee
Linda DiPaolo
Anne Dickerson
Diane E. Dracos
Elaine Dym
Joe Easton
Andrew Falkiewicz
Melinda Farris
Katherine Fernstrom
Wilbur Clinton Fisher, III
Michelle Fort
Andrew Foster
Michael Doud Gill
Devorah Goldburg
Gayla Gordon
Daniel Growney
Lora Lee Gunn
Foster Pierce Harbin, III
Barbara Harris
Dianne Harrison
Jean Hayes
David Herron
John Hines
John Holloway
Karen Hunt
Donald Iloff, Jr.
Ardis Johnson
Lindsey Johnson
Cathleen Justin
Joseph Justin
Karyn Kane
Erich Kimbrough
Paul Kranhold
John La Penta
Deidre Lamppin
Madelyn (Lynn) Lawson
Jane Leo
William C. Lorick
Kathleen Lydon
Dave MacLaughlin
Charles Maloney, III
Jane Manley
Kathleen C. Marion
Shirley Martinez
Candia Mausser
Gregory E. McGinity
John McGinn
Juliette McLennan
Lynn Marie Miller
Edward Monroe
Stephen Monson
Howard Mortman
Ellen Murray
Valerie Musgrove
A. Mark Neuman
Frank Nieves
Michael O'Callaghan
Katherine Oliver
Kevin Parks
Bradley Pirie
Marian Powers
Margueritte Ramos
Altagracia Ramos
Julie Rao
David Reinmund
Brian Rell
Peggy Riley

Richard Rossi
David Sadlier
Drucie Scaling
Neil Schreibner
M. Scott Sears
Claire Sechler
Fernando A. Serpa
Stratford Shields
Jonathan Alex Sloan
Kristen Smallwood
Christopher M. Smith
Rita Solon
Nancy Taffel
Suzanna Tashiro
Jeffrey L. Taylor
Guy Taylor
Shane Tews
Victoria Thornton
Elizabeth Valega
Ann Venture
Jackelyn Viera
Steve Watson
William Wead
Elisabeth Ann Wear
J. Edward Whitehead, Jr.
Erwin Wilcox
Melissa Williams
Lia Zaccagnino
Luke Zahner
Lauren Zanca

Special Events
Kevin E. Moley, *Director*
William Canary, *Deputy Director*
Gary Fendler, *Deputy Director*
Lacey Neuhaus, *Deputy Director*
Judd Swift, *Deputy Director*
Jay Allison
Marilyn Armor
Bradley Blakeman
Mike Brennan
Jonathan Bush
Patricia Cannon
Patricia S. Carlson
Lenny Cherson
Patricia Clarey
Mildred Cooper
Edward Cowling
Anne Csorba
Heather Denison
Daniel B. Denning
Abby Lynn Didrickson
Susan Eckelkamp
Laura Farish
Jane R. Field
Sharon Fitzpatrick
Spencer Geissinger
Elizabeth Gonsoulin
Elizabeth Gordon
Karen Griffin
Patrick Grubbe
Richard Haft
Sydney Hall
Shannon Hamm
Carey O'Kelly Hammett
Marianne Hansen
Elizabeth Harper
Michael Harrell
Alexandra Hemminway
Donna Henderson
John Herrick, Jr.
Katherine Holt
Rebecca Hudson
John Hutchison
Tom Jasien
Nancy Johnson
Margaret Jonas
Lyn D. Kennelly
William (Wally) Kleine
Bruce W. Kletz
Markos P. Koro
Rocky Kuonen
Bruce Mazza Langmaid
Evelyn K. Lanier
Lisa Lasseigne
Liz Laszlo
Stephen Lowry
Douglas MacKenzie
Donald Mains
Paul McAndrew
Trent McGuire
Sally M. McKeag
Joan C. Michel
Debbie Miller
Paul C. Miller

Chris Molineaux
Robert Tipton Moody
Gene Morlan
Leslie J. Novitsky
John Pastuovic
Richard F. Pharr, Jr.
Tracy Presock
Edward Priola
Betty M. Priola
Chris (Tyler) Prochnow
Rosemary Ramirez
George Rasley
Craig Ray
Paula Reano
Suzanne M. Rich
Steven Ross
E. Marice (Rici) Rutkoff
Robert Schuler
Timothy Simonson
Elizabeth Smith
Richard Thomas
Leo Tomeu
Robert (Giles) Tucker
Robert E. Turner, Jr.
Frederick W. Volcansek
Kelly Walker
Ruth Waller
Michael O. Ware
Craig Whitney
Kathy Wills

Tickets
John C. Gartland, *Director*
William Houston, *Deputy Director*
Victoria Hughes, *Deputy Director*
Jeffrey K. Taylor, *Deputy Director*
Lynne Walker, *Deputy Director*
Mary Bailey
Nina Bishop
R. Putnam Coes
Peter Cunningham
Dan Durkin
Diane Greenspun
Paula Hobson
Ann Howard
Bulbul Howard
Peter Johnson
Augustine Long
Sharon McGann
Carrie McKee
Leslie Milsten
J. Michael Rehwaldt
Mark Serrano
Peter Shoemaker
Stephanie Silverman
Karen Timmons

Treasury
J. Stanley Huckaby, *Chief Financial Officer*
William S. Jasien, *Principal Deputy*
Gregory Dofoid, *Deputy Director*
Dorothy Moley, *Deputy Director*
Darlene Riley, *Deputy Director*
Hugh Addington
Gail Albrecht
Bruce A. Alford
Monica Armendariz
Caroline E. Bassett
John Baxter
Robin J. Beard
Eric Gordon Bing
MaryEllen Brown
Robert M. Brown
James Cahill
Martha E. Clement
Craig Conatser
Keith Davis
Stephen Dove
Marianne C. Farnsworth
Dona J. Fendler
Anne Marie Finley
Mary Elizabeth Fritz
Elizabeth Ganzi
Julie Ann Gregg
William Dominic Grote
Brian P. Harrington
James D. Harris
Jeffrey Held
Leslie Hendrix
Rebecca Hill
Zorana Ilic
Ronald W. Imbach, Jr.
Thomas Jenkins
Eric S. Jowett
Sandra Lehrer

Timothy J. Lockhart
Laurie Luhn
Martha Eileen McGreevy
Michael Mendoza
James Mermis
Shaun Miller
Susan Moore
Lillie P. Murdock
Christopher Ott
Lady Josephine Parker
Kimberly A. Rice
Lisa Rogers
Gail Seymour
Marjorie Shaw
Susan C. Shook
Bruce Simon
Frances Spell
Holly Steger
Jocelyn Stevenson
Hilry S. Stroup
Paige C. Tarver
Eric Turner
Deborah Underhill
Holly K. Volatile

Armed Forces Inaugural Committee
Major General Donald C. Hilbert, USA
Brigadier General Julius F. Johnson, USA
Colonel George T. Hudgens, USA

Joint Congressional Committee on Inaugural Ceremonies
Senator Wendell H. Ford, *Chairman*
Senator George J. Mitchell
Senator Ted Stevens
Speaker of the House Jim Wright
Representative Thomas S. Foley
Representative Robert H. Michel
Michael J. Ruehling, *Executive Director*

Inaugural Advisory Committee
Richard F. Hohlt, *Chairman*
Susan E. Alvarado
Haley Barbour
Richard W. Bliss
Red Cavaney
Mitchell E. Daniels, Jr.
William Henkel
Allan B. Hubbard
Mary Jo Jacobi
John G. Keller
Francis X. Lilly
Paul J. Manafort, Jr.
Paul C. Miller
David N. Parker
J. Steven Rhodes
Sherrie Sandy Rollins
Ronald H. Walker

Inaugural Guaranty Fund—1989

Abbott Laboratories
AEtna Life and Casualty Company
Mr. Charles S. Ackerman
Mr. and Mrs. Randolph J. Agley
Mr. and Mrs. Martin L. Allday
Allied-Signal Inc.
Ms. Linda W. Allison
American Bankers Association
American Express Company
American Gas Association
American Home Products Corporation
American Nuclear Energy Council
American Security Bank, N.A.
Amoco Corporation
Amway Corporation
Mr. and Mrs. D.O. Andreas
Anheuser-Busch Companies, Inc.
AOC Management, Inc.
Ashland Oil, Inc.
AT&T
Atlantic Richfield Company
Rabbi Milton Balkany
Bank of America
Mrs. Anne Stuart Batchelder
Mr. Lawrence E. Bathgate, II
Bell Atlantic Corporation
Mr. and Mrs. Charles A. Bird
Mr. and Mrs. H.F. "Bert" Boeckmann, II
Mr. and Mrs. C. Harvey Bradley

Mr. Donald L. Bren
Bristol-Myers Company
Mr. and Mrs. Raymond G. Chambers
Chase Manhattan Corporation
Mr. and Mrs. E.B. Chester, Jr.
Chevron Corporation
Chili's Inc.
Chrysler Corporation
CIGNA Corporation
The Coca-Cola Company
Mr. and Mrs. William L. Collins, III
Communications Satellite Corporation
Compressor Engineering Corporation
Computer Sciences Corporation
ConAgra, Inc.
Copeland, Wickersham, Wiley & Company
Mr. and Mrs. Alec P. Courtelis
Mr. and Mrs. Earle M. Craig, Jr.
Mr. Bill Daniels
Mr. and Mrs. Henri de Compiegne, Jr.
Mr. Frank De Francis
Mr. and Mrs. Charles A. Dean
Mr. and Mrs. Jimmy Dean
Delta Air Lines, Inc.
Dow Chemical U.S.A.
Dow Corning Corporation
Mr. and Mrs. William H. Draper, III
Dresser Industries, Inc.
Edison Electric Institute
Enron Corp.
ENSERCH Corporation
The Equitable Financial Companies
Exxon Corporation
Mr. and Mrs. Jerry E. Finger
Mr. and Mrs. Arthur M. Fischer
Mr. Max M. Fisher
The Honorable and Mrs. William H.G. Fitzgerald
Fluor Corporation
Food Marketing Institute
Mr. Gary S. Frank
Frederick Weisman Company
General Electric Company
Mr. and Mrs. David Harrison Gilmour
The Greyhound Corporation
Mr. Arden R. Grover
Grumman Corporation
Mr. and Mrs. Jack O. Guy
Hallmark Cards, Inc.
Mr. and Mrs. Henry L. Hillman
Dr. Armand Hammer
Mr. and Mrs. R.E. Heckert
Mr. and Mrs. J. Harvey Herd
Mr. and Mrs. Frank D. Hickingbotham
Hills Materials of South Dakota, Stanford Adelstein
Mr. and Mrs. Glen A. Holden
Dorothy Holt Kimsey
Holt Companies, Peter M. Holt
The Home Group, Inc.
Huizenga Holdings, Inc.
Mr. and Mrs. Ray L. Hunt
IBM
Information Services, Inc.
Mr. and Mrs. Fred Israel
J.B. Hunt Transport, Inc.
J.C. Penney Company, Inc.
Johnson & Johnson Family of Companies
Mr. and Mrs. Robert G. Johnson
Mr. Donald G. and Terri L. Jones
Mr. and Mrs. Jerry Jones
Mr. and Mrs. Sheldon B. Kamins
Mr. Arthur and Tichi Wilkerson Kassel
Mr. Jay and Mrs. Jean Kislak
Mr. George Klein
Mr. Alan B. Landis
The Honorable and Mrs. Ronald S. Lauder
Mr. Richard P. Lawless
Mr. and Mrs. Howard W. Long
Mr. Gordon C. Luce
Mr. and Mrs. G. Sage Lyons
Mr. and Mrs. Mark Markarian
Marriott Corporation
Martin Marietta Corporation
McLane Company, Inc.
Mr. and Mrs. Dennis J. McGillicuddy
Mr. James R. McManus
MeraBank, a subsidiary of Pinnacle West Capital Corporation
Merrill Lynch & Co., Inc.
Mitsui & Co. (U.S.A.), Inc.
Mr. and Mrs. George A. Moberly
Mobil Corporation
Mr. and Mrs. James C. Morgan
Mr. David H. Murdock
National Association of Broadcasters
National Association of Home Builders

National Federation of Independent Business
National Intergroup, Inc.
National Soft Drink Association
Mr. Phil R. North
Mr. and Mrs. Peter O'Donnell, Jr.
Pacific Resources, Inc.
Pacific Telesis Group
Mr. and Mrs. Gerald L. Parsky
Pennzoil Company
Mr. and Mrs. Joe Pevehouse
Pharmaceutical Manufacturers Association
Philip Morris Management Corp.
Mr. and Mrs. Jesse Philips
Phillips Petroleum Company
Dr. and Mrs. Ricardo Pines
Mr. and Mrs. Heinz C. Prechter
Mr. and Mrs. Chesley Pruet
Real Properties, Inc.
R.G. Barry Corporation
R.J. Reynolds Tobacco
Mr. and Mrs. Winthrop P. Rockefeller
Roger & Wells/Victor Ganzi
Dr. and Mrs. Walter E. Rudisch
Mr. and Mrs. Richard Sambol
Sandoz Corporation
Santarelli, Carroccio, Hannaford, Farrell & Mack
Mr. and Mrs. B. Francis Saul, II
Mr. Charles Schulze & Mr. Jerry Blum
Sears, Roebuck & Co.
Second National Federal Savings Bank
Security Tag Systems, Inc.
Mr. Peter W. Senopoulos, Gallagher and Gallagher, C.P.
Ms. Therese M. Shaheen
Mr. J. Gary Shansby
Shell Oil Company
Mr. Jeffrey and Mrs. Joy Silverman
Mr. and Mrs. James P. Simmons
Mr. and Mrs. Van P. Smith
Southwestern Bell Corporation— Washington, Inc.
Mr. and Mrs. Alex G. Spanos
Squibb Corporation
Stephens Inc.
Mr. and Mrs. Donald R. Stephens
Sullivan Development Co., Inc.
Sun Company, Inc.
Sun-Diamond Growers of California
Sun Exploration & Production Company
Mr. and Mrs. John J. Tedesco
Tenneco Inc.
Textron Inc.
3M
Mr. and Mrs. Jonathan M. Tisch
The Tobacco Institute
Torchmark Corporation
Triangle Industries, Inc.
The Honorable and Mrs. Carlton E. Turner
Union Carbide Corporation
United Airlines
United States League of Savings Institutions
United Technologies
UNOCAL
USAir, Inc.
USX Corporation
Mr. and Mrs. Tomas Vara
Mr. Leopoldo F. Villareal
Waste Management Inc.
Mr. John Giffen Weinmann
Mr. and Mrs. Jerry C. Weintraub
Wiley, Rein and Fielding
Mr. and Mrs. Earle C. Williams
Mr. and Mrs. Gene Willingham
Mr. and Mrs. James J. Wilson
Mr. and Mrs. William Wilson, III
Mr. and Mrs. Richard D. Wood

Honorary Inaugural Chairmen

Mr. and Mrs. B. B. Andersen
Mrs. Flora Atherton
The Honorable and Mrs. Lee Atwater
The Honorable Jeanie Austin
The Honorable and Mrs. James A. Baker, III
Mr. and Mrs. Samuel Barshop
Mr. and Mrs. Carter Beese
Mr. and Mrs. Fitzgerald Bemiss
The Honorable and Mrs. William J. Bennett
The Honorable Shirley Temple Black
Mrs. Wallace Boyd
Mr. and Mrs. C. Harvey Bradley
The Honorable and Mrs. Nicholas E. Brady

The Honorable and Mrs. W. Lyons Brown, Jr.
The Honorable and Mrs. Edward Broyhill
Mr. and Mrs. Marvin Bush
Mrs. Prescott Bush, Sr.
The Honorable and Mrs. Henry Edward Catto, Jr.
The Honorable and Mrs. Lauro F. Cavazos
Mr. Wilt Chamberlain
Mr. and Mrs. C. Fred Chambers
Mrs. John E. Chapoton
Mrs. Masten Childers
Mr. and Mrs. James Click
Mr. and Mrs. Alec Courtelis
Mr. and Mrs. Paul Coverdell
Mr. and Mrs. Trammell Crow
The Honorable and Mrs. Edward J. Derwinski
The Honorable Elizabeth Hanford Dole and the Honorable Robert J. Dole
Mr. and Mrs. William Farish, III
Mr. and Mrs. Max M. Fisher
Mr. and Mrs. Walter J. Ganzi
Mr. and Mrs. Bruce Gelb
Mr. and Mrs. Howard Goldenfarb
Mr. and Mrs. Allan Green
Mr. and Mrs. Richard E. Greer
Mr. and Mrs. Donald J. Hall
The Honorable Margaret Hance
Mrs. Willard Heminway
The Honorable and Mrs. James Hewgley, Jr.
Mr. William H. Heyman
Mr. and Mrs. Henry L. Hillman
Mrs. Bobby Holt
Mr. Bob Hope
Mr. and Mrs. Raymond Hunt
Mr. J. Howard Johnson
The Honorable and Mrs. Jack F. Kemp
Mr. and Mrs. George Kettle
Mr. Fritz-Alan Korth
Mr. and Mrs. Henry R. Kravis
Ms. Cheryl Ladd
Ms. Deborah Leighton
Mr. and Mrs. Hugh Liedtke
Mr. and Mrs. William C. Liedtke, III
The Honorable and Mrs. Manuel Lujan, Jr.
Mr. and Mrs. Sage Lyons
Mrs. William McKenzie
Mr. and Mrs. Colin McMillan
The Honorable and Mrs. William Milliken
The Honorable and Mrs. Robert A. Mosbacher
Mr. William Moss
Mr. and Mrs. William R. Neale
Mrs. DeWitt Neighbors
Mr. Chuck Norris
Mrs. Marvin Pierce
Mrs. James Shelley Percy
Mr. and Mrs. George Pfau
Mr. and Mrs. Russell S. Reynolds, Jr.
Mr. Don Rhodes
Mr. and Mrs. Mel Sembler
Mr. and Mrs. Peter Senopoulos
The Honorable Samuel Knox Skinner
Mrs. Jonathan Sloat
Mr. and Mrs. Roger Staubach
Mr. Jack Steel
Mr. and Mrs. Jack Stevens
Mrs. Potter Stewart
Mrs. Stephen M. Studdert
The Honorable and Mrs. Louis W. Sullivan
The Honorable and Mrs. John H. Sununu
The Honorable and Mrs. Richard Thornburgh
The Honorable John G. Tower
Admiral and Mrs. James D. Watkins, USN (Ret.)
Mr. and Mrs. Jerry Weintraub
Mr. and Mrs. Ted Welch
Brigadier General Chuck Yeager, USAF (Ret.)
The Honorable and Mrs. Clayton Yeutter
Mr. and Mrs. Joseph Zappala

Corporate Sponsors

Adolph Coors Company
Allied-Signal Inc.
American Bankers Association
American Concrete Pipe Association
American Cafe
American Financial Corporation
American Honda Motor Co., Inc.
American Recreation Coalition
American Express Company
American Society of Florists
Amoco Corporation
Amway Corporation
Andrews Bartlett
Angelo Bonita/Washington Harbor
Anheuser-Busch Companies, Inc.
Archer Daniels Midland Company

139

ARCO
Apple Computers, Inc.
Armand's Pizza
Artesia Waters, Inc.
Ashland Oil, Inc.
AT&T
Atlantic and Pacific Tea Company
Atlantic Richfield Company
B & B Washington's Caterer
Batus Industries
B.C.E. Corporation
Bell Atlantic Corporation
Binney and Smith Corporation
The Boston Popcorn Company
Bread and Chocolate Company
Bristol-Myers Company
Britches of Georgetown
Brown and Forman Beverage Company
Brown, Williamson Tobacco Corporation
Budget Rent-a-Car
Caliante Chile, Inc.
Thomas Cantomiri's and Sons
Capitol View Catering, Inc.
Chateau-Potelle Winery
Chateau St. Michelle
Christian and Company Entertainment
Christini's
Chrysler Motor Company
Citicorp/Citibank
The Coca-Cola Company
CompuCom Systems, Inc.
Computer Sciences Corporation
ConAgra, Inc.
Consolidated Natural Gas Company
Contemp Vans
Copeland, Wickersham, Wiley & Co., Inc.
Department of the Interior
Design Cuisine Caterers
Dresser Industries, Inc.
E. I. du Pont de Nemours & Co.
J. Fred Dual and Associates
Duke Zeiberts Restaurant
Eastman Kodak Company
Electronic Industries Association
Enron Corporation
Exxon Corporation
Falcon Microsystems
Farley Industries
Mr. Simon Fireman
The Freeman Company
The French Market
Ford Motor Company
Food Marketing Institute
Frost Lighting
Fleetwood Enterprises
Garfinckel's
General Electric Company
General Motors Corporation
Giant Food Inc.
Glorious Foods
Gold Office Products
Goodmark Foods, Inc.
Great Lakes Financial
The Greenbrier
The Greyhound Corporation
Hal Diamond Magic Show
Hallmark Cards, Inc.
Earl C. Hargrove and Hargrove, Inc.
Heron, Burchette, Ruckert & Rothwell
Heublein Inc.
The Home Group, Inc.
Houston Sports
Huizenga Holdings, Inc.
Hunt Oil
Independent Stave Company
Indiana Chamber of Commerce
IBM
The International Brotherhood of Teamsters
The Irvine Company
J. B. Hunt Transport, Inc.
J. C. Penney Company, Inc.
Jack Daniels Distillery
Johnson & Johnson Family of Companies
King World Features
Kodalux Processing
Korbel
Korn/Ferry International
Kraft, Inc.
M&M Mars
Machiavelli's
Anthony Maglica, MAG Instruments, Inc.
Management Systems Applications
Marriott Corporation
McDonald's
Merrill Lynch & Company, Inc.

Mesa Limited Partnership
Don Mischer Productions
Mobil Oil Corporation
Moet Hennessy, U.S. Corporation
Phillip Morris, Inc.
Motorola
MSA, Inc.
Must Software International
NEC Home Electronics
David Nash Productions
National Air and Space Museum
National Park Service
National Intergroup, Inc.
National Soft Drink Association
Naval Air Training Command Choir
Necco Candy Cupboard
Northrop Corporation
Nosegay Florists
Novell, Inc.
Oracle Complex Systems
Old Town Trolley Tours
Pace Foods
Pacific Telesis Group
Panafax
Paralyzed Veterans of America
Pepsi-Cola and Pepsi-Cola Bottlers
    of Washington, D.C.
Pfizer, Inc.
Pier Seven Restaurant
Pizza Movers
Pindar Vineyards
Herbie Plankenton/Flowers, Plants and Gardens
Popeye's
P.R. Inc.
Prudential Insurance Company of America
Public Entertainment Association for Culture
    and Education
Qui-Bell Mineral Water
Revlon, Inc.
R. J. Reynolds Tobacco
Richardson After Dinner Mints
Ridgewells Caterer
Roma Restaurant
Rockwell International
Ryder Systems, Inc.
Safeway
Sambol Construction Corporation
Samsung Information Systems
Sandoz Corporation
Santarelli, Carroccio, Hannaford, Farrell & Mack
Saratoga Water
Sears, Roebuck & Co.
Service America Corporation
Shell Oil Company
Smithsonian Institution
Smithsonian Office of Horticulture
Smithsonian Office of Photography
Snyder-Hixon
Society of American Florists
Southwestern Bell Corporation
Star Craft Corporation
V. Coke Stuart, Sr.
Sunweave Linen Corporation
Sun Company, Inc.
Sun-Diamond Growers of California
SynOptics Communications
Tandy Corporation
TeleGraphics, Inc.
Tenneco Inc.
Textron Inc.
Time-Life Corporation
3M
The Tobacco Institute
Torchmark Corporation
Triangle Industries, Inc.
Tysons Corner Center
United Airlines
United Technologies Corporation
USAA
UST
US Tobacco/St. Genevieve Wines
US West Corporation
USO-Metropolitan Washington
Don Vanderbrook Florists, Inc.
Wagner and Brown
Walt Disney Productions
Washington Board of Trade
Washington Convention Center
    Board of Directors
Washington Metropolitan Area Transit Authority
Waste Management Inc.
Waverly, a division of F. Schumacher
    and Company
Mr. Frederick Weisman
Wesray Capital Corporation

Windows Catering Company
Wing Master's Grill
The Wonder Company
Woodward and Lothrop
Charlotte Woolard
Xerox Corporation

American Presidential Pageant

Mr. and Mrs. Roger Staubach, Chairmen

Committee
Mr. Robert O. Aders
The Honorable Randolph Agley
Mr. Howard P. Allen
Mr. DeLonne Anderson
The Honorable Hushang Ansary
The Honorable Victor Atiyeh
Mr. Earl Baker
The Honorable J. Glenn Beall
Mr. John C. Bierwirth
Mr. Roger A. Bodman
Mr. Dick G. Boerger
Mr. James H. Brennan
Mr. H. R. Bright
Mr. Norman Brinker
The Honorable James Broyhill
Mr. Joel Broyhill
Mr. Howard Callaway
The Honorable Bill Campbell
Mr. Lane Carson
Mr. Raymond G. Chambers
The Honorable Larry Cobb
Mr. Fred Cooper
The Honorable Diana Cox
Mr. Frank Crawford
Mr. Jim Crawford
Mr. Bill Daniels
Mr. Steven Dart
Mr. Roy Demmon
Mr. Lewis Donaldson
Mr. John T. Dorrance
The Honorable Lee S. Dreyfus
Mr. Myron Du Bain
Mr. Wyatt Durrette
Ms. Martha Edens
Mr. Donald Evans
Mr. James L. Ferguson
Mr. Tom Fowler
The Honorable Robert Franks
Mr. James E. Fuchs
Mr. Jack E. Galt
Mr. Richard Glanton
The Honorable Mills E. Goodwin
Mr. Harold Goldberg
Mr. Roy M. Goodman
Mr. Bill Graham
Mr. George Graham
Mr. Alex Grass
Mr. Harry Gray
Mr. Michael Grebe
The Honorable John Grenier
Mr. Richard J. Guggenheim
Mr. Charles L. Hardwick
Mr. Barry Harris
Mr. Andrew D. Hart, Jr.
Mr. Larry Haynes
Mr. James Helzer
Mr. Paul Hicks
The Honorable Paul Hillegonds
The Honorable Lawrence J. Hogan
Mr. and Mrs. Peter Hurtgen
Mr. R. L. Ireland, III
The Honorable William Janklow
The Honorable Dave Johnson
Mrs. J. Howard Johnson
Mr. Thomas J. Judge
Mr. Wilhelm C. Kast
Mr. John King
Mr. Seymour H. Knox, III
Mr. Ken Lay
Mr. Howard H. Leach
The Honorable Robert List
Mr. John D. Macomber
Mr. Donald R. Margo, II
Mr. Peter Marks
The Honorable Benjamin Marsh
Mr. Louis Marx
Mr. Wells McCurdy
Mr. John McGoff
The Honorable Brian McKay
Mr. James R. McManus
Mr. Tom Mechler
The Honorable Walter Dale Miller
Mr. Joseph N. Mondello

Mr. Jack Moseley
Mr. John Munger
Mr. David Murdoch
Ms. Bernice Murray
Ms. Della Newman
Mrs. Sally Novetzke
Mr. John D. Ong
The Honorable L. Brooks Patterson
Mr. Milton Petrie
Mr. Charles Pickering
Mr. David Place
Mr. Ronald D. Ray
Mr. J. Ronald Reeves
Dr. Jay S. Reibel
Mr. Anthony Salinas
Mr. Richard Sambol
Mr. Hillard Selk
Mr. J. Gary Shansby
Mr. and Mrs. Jim Simmons
Mr. W. Laird Stabler
The Honorable Don Stitt
The Honorable Ted Strickland
Mr. Jonathan T. Swain
Mrs. Barbara Taylor
Mr. Richard P. Taylor
Mr. John J. Tedesco
Mr. Jon Thomas
The Honorable Liz Thomas
The Honorable Charles Thone
Mr. Brian P. Tierney
Mr. George D. Webster
Mr. John G. Weinmann
Mr. George H. Weyerhaeuser
The Honorable John C. Whitehead
Mrs. Eunice B. Whittlesey
Mr. David K. Wilson
Mrs. Frederick R. H. Witherby
Mr. and Mrs. Dalton Woods
The Honorable Charles Yob
Mr. Morris E. Zukerman

Bob Johnson, Producer
Mark Murray, Producer

An American Tribute to Democracy

Committee
Dr. and Mrs. Steven Beering
Dr. and Mrs. Gerald L. Bepko
Dr. and Mrs. Robert G. Bottoms
The Honorable and Mrs. Otis R. Bowen
The Honorable and Mrs. Dan Burton
The Honorable and Mrs. Daniel Coats
Mr. and Mrs. Thomas Ehrlich
Dr. and Mrs. Eugene Habeker
The Honorable and Mrs. Lee H. Hamilton
Professor and Mrs. William S. Harvey
Father Theodore Hesburgh
The Honorable and Mrs. John Hiler
The Honorable and Mrs. Andrew Jacobs, Jr.
The Honorable Jim Jontz
The Honorable and Mrs. Alan L. Keyes
The Honorable Jeane J. Kirkpatrick
    and Dr. Kirkpatrick
The Honorable and Mrs. Richard G. Lugar
Father Edward Malloy
Mr. and Mrs. William B. Martin
The Honorable and Mrs. Frank McCloskey
The Honorable Ann McLaughlin
The Honorable and Mrs. John T. Myers
The Honorable and Mrs. Robert Orr
The Honorable and Mrs. Richard N. Perle
Mr. and Mrs. Chris Schenkel
The Honorable and Mrs. Philip R. Sharp
The Honorable and Mrs. Jose S. Sorzano
The Honorable and Mrs. Peter J. Visclosky

Entertainment
Mr. James MacArthur, Master of Ceremonies
Mr. Wilford Brimley
The Honorable Robert H. Michel
Mr. Greg Morris
The Mormon Tabernacle Choir
The United States Air Force Band
The United States Air Force Singing Sergeants

Inaugural Ball

Mrs. John E. Chapoton
1989 Inaugural Ball Chairman

Kennedy Center

General Chairmen
The Honorable and Mrs. William H. Draper, III

Mr. and Mrs. Joseph Bernard Gildenhorn

Committee
The Honorable and Mrs. John R. Alison,
 Co-Chairmen
Mr. Marshall B. Coyne and Mrs. Jane
 Gordon Coyne, Co-Chairmen
Mr. and Mrs. Gordon Zacks, Co-Chairmen
The Honorable and Mrs. Willis C. Armstrong
The Honorable Barbara Franklin Barnes
 and Mr. Wallace Barnes
Mr. and Mrs. John Behrendt
Mr. and Mrs. Stuart Bernstein
The Honorable and Mrs. Frederick M. Bush
The Honorable and Mrs. Henry Catto
The Honorable and Mrs. William Curley
The Honorable Diana Lady Dougan and
 Mr. J. Lynn Dougan
Mr. and Mrs. Michael Gildenhorn
Mr. and Mrs. F. P. Johnson, Jr.
Mr. and Mrs. Samuel Kaminsky
Mr. and Mrs. Paul Lambert
The Honorable and Mrs. David Schiverick Smith

Music
Michael Carney Orchestra
Ed Gerlach Orchestra
Strolling Strings

National Air and Space Museum

General Chairmen
The Honorable and Mrs. Robert L. Clarke
Mrs. Alice H. Taussig

Committee
Mr. and Mrs. B.Z. Lee, Co-Chairmen
Mr. and Mrs. Joe Lewis Albritton
Mr. and Mrs. J. Evans Attwell
Mr. and Mrs. Nathan Avery
Mr. and Mrs. Daniel Breen
The Honorable and Mrs. O. Donaldson Chapoton
Mr. and Mrs. Hal DeMoss
Mr. and Mrs. Wayne Gibbens
The Honorable and Mrs. Lawrence B. Gibbs
Mr. and Mrs. Arthur Grace
Mr. and Mrs. Donald Gregg
Ms. Margaret Alison Gregg and
 Mr. Thaxter Robert Sharp
Mr. and Mrs. Arden Berkeley Judd, Jr.
The Honorable Edward W. Kelley, Jr.
Mrs. Joanne Lawson and Mr. Thomas T. Stohlman
Dr. and Mrs. William Manger
The Honorable and Mrs. Jan W. Mares
Ms. Diane Morales and Mr. Robert Morales
Mr. and Mrs. Phillip R. Roof
The Honorable and Mrs. Marion Smoak

Music
Bill Harrington Orchestra
Nighthawks Orchestra
Preservation Hall Jazz Band
Strolling Strings
Princeton Footnotes

Omni Shoreham

General Chairmen
Mr. and Mrs. Edwin Lyon Dale, Jr.
The Honorable and Mrs. L. Ebersole Gaines

Committee
Mrs. Nina Antorsky
Mr. and Mrs. Charles DiBona
Mrs. Yves Dujandin
Mr. and Mrs. John D. Ferguson
Ms. Anne Mackle
Mrs. Patricia Patterson
Dr. and Mrs. David Peyton
Ms. Pat Robbie
The Honorable and Mrs. Stuart W. Rockwell
The Honorable and Mrs. William D. Ruckelshaus
Mr. and Mrs. B. Francis Saul, II
The Honorable and Mrs. Ivan Selin
Mr. and Mrs. Michael R. Stanfield
The Honorable and Mrs. William Verity

Music
Drew Corcoran Orchestra
Lester Lanin Orchestra
Blues Alley Jazz Quintet

Pension Building

General Chairmen
The Honorable and Mrs. Craig A. Nalen
Mr. and Mrs. John Ely Pflieger

Committee
Mr. and Mrs. Spencer Davis
The Honorable and Mrs. John Eden
Mr. and Mrs. William Gorog
Mr. and Mrs. Brandon Grove
Mrs. Margaret Hodges
Mr. and Mrs. James Holman
Mr. and Mrs. Kempton Jenkins
Mr. and Mrs. Freeborn Garrettson Jewett, Jr.
Mr. and Mrs. Ernest Nugent May
Mr. and Mrs. John Pflieger
Mr. and Mrs. Philip W. Pillsbury, Jr.

Music
Buddy Brock Orchestra
Woody Herman Orchestra

Sheraton Washington Hotel

General Chairmen
The Honorable and Mrs. Charles Camalier, Jr.
Mr. and Mrs. Anthony John Thompson

Committee
Mr. and Mrs. David Bruce Amiot
Mr. and Mrs. John Laing Bowles
Mr. and Mrs. Charles A. Camalier, III
Mr. F. Davis Camalier
Mr. and Mrs. Phillip A. Campbell
Dr. and Mrs. James Foster
Ms. Delores Arline Harper
Mr. and Mrs. Jonathan Hunt
Mr. and Mrs. William Lilley, II
Dr. and Mrs. Keith M. Lindgren
Mr. Peter James McGee
Miss Sarah McGovern
Mr. and Mrs. Lawrence Wiley Secrest, III
Mr. and Mrs. James Joseph Tansey

Music
Billy Lang/Sounds of Glenn Miller Orchestra
Floating Opera

Union Station

General Chairmen
The Honorable and Mrs. Dean Burch
Mr. and Mrs. William Lewis Slover

Committee
Mr. and Mrs. Roger Emsellem
Mrs. Laurie G. Firestone
Mr. and Mrs. Robert Flinn
Mr. and Mrs. Robert Goodkind
Mr. Ronald Grimaldi
Mr. and Mrs. James G. Lang
Mrs. Jane Lorentzen
Mr. and Mrs. John W. Mettler, III
Mr. and Mrs. Herbert Porter
Miss Elizabeth B. Slover
Miss Sarah Slover
Mr. William L. Slover, Jr.
Mr. and Mrs. John Sower
Mr. Alan Tanksley
Mr. and Mrs. Bruce Thompson
Mr. Todd Vaughan

Music
Gene Donati Orchestra
Neal Smith Orchestra
Teo & New York Blue All Stars

Washington Convention Center Stars

General Chairmen
The Honorable and Mrs. Davis Robinson
Mr. and Mrs. Jonathan Sloat

Committee
Mr. and Mrs. Raymond J. Howar, Co-Chairmen
Mr. and Mrs. Gene Perry Bono
Mr. and Mrs. E. Edward Bruce
Ms. Mary Byrnes
Mr. and Mrs. Scott Campbell
Mr. and Mrs. Charles Carroll Carter
Mr. and Mrs. Roy Demmon
Mr. and Mrs. C. William Dyke
Mr. and Mrs. Arthur A. Fletcher
Mr. and Mrs. John D. Garst, Jr.

The Reverend and Mrs. Jerry Moore
Dr. and Mrs. W. Tabb Moore
Mr. and Mrs. Hobart Porter
Mr. and Mrs. Stephen D. Potts
Mr. and Mrs. Edward M. Prince
Mr. and Mrs. Michael Rollyson
Mr. and Mrs. Ray Scully
Mr. and Mrs. James W. Singer, III
Mr. and Mrs. R. Kenly Webster

Music
Jack Morton Orchestra
Lionel Hampton Orchestra
Bob Dini Orchestra
Sam Schrieber Orchestra

Washington Convention Center Stripes

General Chairmen
Mr. and Mrs. Robert Elliott Freer, Jr.
Mrs. Carla Scheidker Levesque

Committee
Mr. and Mrs. Michael Adams
Mr. and Mrs. Francis W. Cash
Mr. Sheldon Clark, II
Mr. and Mrs. Sterling D. Colton
Mr. John Damgard
Mr. and Mrs. Mitchell Drake
Ms. Kimberly Freer
Mr. and Mrs. James E. Fuchs
The Honorable and Mrs. John C. Gartland
Mr. and Mrs. Fred T. Goldberg, Jr.
Mr. and Mrs. Smith Hempstone
The Honorable Robert J. Horn and the
 Honorable Marian Rose Blank
Mr. and Mrs. Richard J. Knop
Mr. and Mrs. Harvey C. Koch
Mr. and Mrs. John J. McCloy, II
Mr. and Mrs. Frank H. Menaker, Jr.
Mr. and Mrs. Jacques C. Nordeman
Mr. and Mrs. Carl E. Scheidker
Mr. and Mrs. Charles H. Seilheimer, Jr.
Mrs. Sarah H. Smith
Miss Pamela Somers and Mr. Stuart M. Gerson
Mr. and Mrs. Howard B. Wentz, III
Mr. Robert Blough Wentz
Ms. Amanda Williams
Mr. and Mrs. Wesley S. Williams, Jr.

Music
Bob Hardwick Orchestra
Artie Shaw Orchestra
Tony Kelley and the Royal Ambassadors

Washington Hilton

General Chairmen
Mr. and Mrs. Thomas J. Quigley
Mr. and Mrs. Andrew Jackson Somerville, Jr.

Committee
Mr. and Mrs. Andrew Jackson Somerville, III,
 Co-Chairmen
General and Mrs. James Abrahamson
Mr. and Mrs. Arnold Aldrick
Mr. and Mrs. Philip H.M. Beauregard
Mr. and Mrs. Paul Elicker
Mr. and Mrs. Robert Fogarty
Mr. and Mrs. David Fowler
Mr. and Mrs. Steven Hayes
Mr. and Mrs. George Huguely
Mr. and Mrs. Daniel Korengold
Mr. and Mrs. John J. Kirlin
Mr. and Mrs. Steven Nohowel
Mr. and Mrs. Robert Ourisman
Dr. and Mrs. John Queenan
Miss Joan Quigley
Mr. Thomas Quigley, Jr.
Mr. and Mrs. James Rosebush
Mr. and Mrs. Richard Kyle Samperton
Mr. and Mrs. Charles Somerville
Mr. Scott Somerville and Ms. Kathy Tibbits

Music
Peter Duchin Orchestra with Denny Leroux
Ronnie Kole Jazz Orchestra
Pia Zadora and Orchestra

Young Americans' Ball

Host Committee
Mr. James Altmeyer
Mr. Dave Carney

Ms. Christy Casteel
Mr. Leonard S. Coleman, Jr.
The Honorable James A. Courter
Mr. John C. Flanigan
The Honorable Dave Frohnmayer
Ms. Carolyn Gates
Mr. H. P. Goldfield
The Honorable Ken Hollis, Jr.
Mr. George F. Kettle
Mr. Arthur B. Laffer
Ms. Gratia Lousma
Mr. Jack Lousma
Mr. Brian Lungren
The Honorable Robert Marsh
The Honorable Barbara Morrison
Mr. C. Gregg Petersmeyer
Mr. Scott Sewell
The Honorable R. Timothy Shaffer
Mrs. Margaret S. Soter
Mr. Charles J. Urstadt
Mr. Gene Ward
Ms. Barbara Zartman

Music
The Busboys
The Jets
Kid Creole and the Coconuts
The Malemen
The Mo Jo Blues Band
Moe Bandy

Celebration for Young Americans
Howell Begle, Executive Producer
David J. Nash, Producer

Entertainers
Lee Atwater
Joe Cocker
Albert Collins
Steve Cropper
Bo Diddley
Willie Dixon
Donald "Duck" Dunn
Anton Fig
Eddie Floyd
Debby Hastings
Chuck Jackson
Etta James
Dr. John
Lafayette Leake
Cash McCall
Delbert McClinton
Sam Moore
The New Jersey Horns
Billy Preston
James Robertson
Percy Sledge
Koko Taylor
Carla Thomas
Michael Toles
Jimmie Vaughan
Stevie Ray Vaughan and Double Trouble
Joe Louis Walker
Ron Wood

Inaugural Dinner

Corcoran Gallery

Chairmen
Mr. and Mrs. John Davis Firestone
Mrs. James Daniel Theberge

Music
Peter Duchin Orchestra
Strolling Strings

Pension Building

Chairmen
Val Cook
Aniko Gaal
The Honorable and Mrs. Leonard
 Lewis Silverstein

Music
Bill Harrington Orchestra

Union Station

Chairmen
Mr. and Mrs. Charles Thomas Cudlip
Dr. and Mrs. Henry Tucker Dalton
Mr. Bruce C. Ellis
Mr. Jeffrey Ellis

Music
Michael Carney Orchestra

Committee Members
Mr. and Mrs. Michael L. Ainslie
Mr. and Mrs. B.B. Andersen
Mr. and Mrs. Phelps Anderson
The Honorable and Mrs. Dwayne Andreas
Dr. and Mrs. Joseph Steven Ayers
Mrs. Anne Batchelder
Mr. and Mrs. Lawrence Bathgate, III
Mr. and Mrs. Carter Beese
Mr. and Mrs. K. K. Bigelow
Mr. and Mrs. Henry Bloch
Mr. and Mrs. C. Harvey Bradley
The Honorable and Mrs. James A. Brady
The Honorable and Mrs. William E. Brock, III
Mr. and Mrs. Michael L. Browne
Mr. and Mrs. Michael Calvin
Mr. and Mrs. Spofford Canfield
Mr. and Mrs. E. B. Chester
Mr. and Mrs. Lodrick Cook
Mr. Edwin L. Cox, Sr.
Mr. and Mrs. Earle Craig
The Honorable and Mrs. Walter J. P. Curley
Mr. and Mrs. Steven Dart
Mr. and Mrs. Jimmy Dean
The Honorable and Mrs. Kenneth Duberstein
Mr. and Mrs. Donald Duncan
The Honorable and Mrs. Pierre S. du Pont, IV
The Honorable and Mrs. Frank Fahrenkopf
The Honorable and Mrs. Michael R. Farley
The Honorable and Mrs. Michael Galvin
Mr. and Mrs. Victor Ganzi
Mr. and Mrs. Roberto C. Goizueta
Mr. and Mrs. Howard A. Goldenfarb
Mr. and Mrs. Jack Guy
The Honorable and Mrs. Armand Hammer
Mr. and Mrs. Glen A. Holden
Mr. and Mrs. Ray Hunt
Mr. and Mrs. Ronald Kendall
Mrs. Dorothy Holt Kimsey
Mrs. Jewel S. Lafontant
The Honorable and Mrs. Drew Lewis
The Honorable and Mrs. Gordon C. Luce
Mr. and Mrs. Sage Lyons
Mr. Knox McConnell
General and Mrs. Robert McDermott
Mr. and Mrs. Anthony Maglica
Mr. and Mrs. Harris Masterson, III
Mr. and Mrs. David Murdoch
The Honorable and Mrs. Peter O'Donnell, Jr.
The Honorable and Mrs. George Pillsbury
Mr. and Mrs. Heinz Prechter
The Honorable and Mrs. Chesley Pruet
Mr. and Mrs. Robert H. Quenon
The Honorable and Mrs. Richard Richards
Mr. and Mrs. Dean William Roach
Mr. and Mrs. Walter Rudd
Mr. and Mrs. Karl Samuelian
Mr. and Mrs. Jeffrey Silverman
Mr. and Mrs. James P. Simmons
Mr. and Mrs. Joshua I. Smith
Mr. and Mrs. Alexander Spanos
The Honorable and Mrs. John Stabile
Mr. and Mrs. Leland Thompson, Jr.
Mr. and Mrs. W. R. Timken, Jr.
Mr. and Mrs. Wheelock Whitney
Mr. and Mrs. Gene Willingham
Mr. and Mrs. Gordon Zachs
The Honorable and Mrs. Frederick Zeder

Lauren Childress, Dinner Coordinator
Nancy Harvey Steorts, Dinner Coordinator

Inaugural Gala

The Honorable Joseph W. Canzeri, Chairman
Don Mischer, Producer
David J. Goldberg, Co-Producer
Walter Miller, Director
Howell Begle, Coordinating Producer
Peter Matz, Music Director
Bob Keene, Production Designer
Pete Menefee, Costume Designer
Kristine Fernandez, Script Supervisor
John Bradley, Production Supervisor
John Field, Technical Director
Buz Kohan, Writer
Bill Bracken, Associate Producer
Nina Lederman, Associate Producer
Alan Johnson, Choreographer
Bill Klages, Lighting Director
Danetie Herman, Talent Executive
Maureen Kelly, Assistant to Producers
Glen Stickley, Production Manager
Doug Nelson, Audio

Performers
Evelyn Ashford
Anita Baker
Hinton Battle
Brian Boitano
Gregg Burge
Nell Carter
Michael Crawford
Walter Cronkite
Michael Davis
Clint Eastwood
Eastern High School Blue and
   White Marching Machine
Janet Evans
Crystal Gayle
Idaho Jr. Jammer Fiddlers
Julio Iglesias
Susan Jaffe
Joint Services Honor Guard
Kentucky Country
Francis Scott Key, Jr.
Dale Kristien
Cheryl Ladd
Cissie Lynn
Loretta Lynn
Yo Yo Ma
Mormon Tabernacle Choir
Chuck Norris
Oak Ridge Boys
Roberta Peters
Arnold Schwarzenegger
Frank Sinatra
Randy Travis
Tommy Tune
The United States Army Herald Trumpets
United States Naval Academy Glee Club
White Eagle
Peggy Sue Wright
General Chuck Yeager, USAF (Ret.)

George to George

Committee
The Honorable Shirley Temple Black, Chairman
The Honorable Woody Allen
Ms. Anne B. Anstine
Mrs. Ann Ascher
Dr. Bernard M. Barrett, Jr.
Mr. Garrett D. Bowne, IV
The Honorable Leanna Brown
Ms. Rita Dimartino
Ms. Debbie Fields
Mrs. Margaret Garcia
Mr. Christopher T. Heffelfinger
Mr. John A. Love
Mr. Bill Lucas
Mrs. Evelyn Lucas
Mrs. Evelyn McPhail
The Honorable Tony Meeker
Mrs. Mindy Meiklejohn
Mr. Linwood Palmer
Ms. Claris Poppert
Mr. Ranny Reicker
Mr. Randy Ruppert
Mr. Peter Terpuluk
Mr. George F. T. Yancey, Jr.

Robert Johnson, Producer

Entertainers
Arlington Virginia Elementary Show Choir
Big Bird and Maria
Christian the Magician
Cloggers USA
Garray and Tomio's "Cowboy Pickle and
   the Rinky Dinks"
Rachel Graham
Hal Diamond Magic Show
Nicolo the Juggler
The Patriots of Northern Virginia
   Colonial Regiment
Third United States Infantry "The Old Guard"
The United States Coast Guard Band
The United States Navy Sea Chanters Choir

The Inaugural Opening Celebration

Committee
Mr. J. Patrick Barrett
Mr. B. F. Biaggini
Mr. Donald L. Bren
Mrs. Catherine Caldwell Cabaniss
The Honorable A. Paul Cellucci
Mr. Charles L. Creagin
The Honorable John Engler
The Honorable Joseph S. Farland
The Honorable J. Brian Gaffney
Mr. Lionel Hampton

Mr. Tim Hayward
Mr. Harry R. King
Mr. Kenneth G. Langone
Mr. Jack Laugherty
Mr. Gordon C. Luce
Mr. John MacIver
The Honorable Charles McC. Mathias
Mr. W. H. Meadowcroft
The Honorable Ronna Romney
The Honorable and Mrs. Phillip Ruppe
Mr. Bernard Shanley
The Honorable Newton I. Steers, Jr.

Entertainment
Mr. Willard Scott, Master of Ceremonies
America Sings
The Beach Boys
The Gatlin Brothers
The Jets
Lee Greenwood
Sandi Patti
The United States Navy Band
The United States Army Gold Knights Parachute
   Team
Up With People

Inaugural Parade

Committee
The Honorable Caldwell Butler
Mr. Howard Dana
The Honorable and Mrs. Emory Folmar
Mr. and Mrs. Steven French
The Honorable Ruth Griffin
Mr. Andy Guest
Mr. Michael T. Halbouty
The Honorable Robert Jaeckle
Mr. Fritz-Alan Korth
The Honorable Kenneth Kraemer
Mr. John M. Lindley, III
Mr. and Mrs. Bill Lucas
Mr. and Mrs. Wales Madden, Sr.
Mr. Jack Marshall
Mr. Steve Merksamer
The Honorable Natalie Meyer
Mr. Art Modell
The Honorable Sue Myrick
The Honorable Louie Nunn
Ms. Edwina Prior
The Honorable James Rhodes
The Honorable William Saltonstall
Mr. Bob Schroeder
Mr. Peter Secchia
The Honorable Reginald J. Smith
Mr. Joseph A. Sullivan
The Honorable and Mrs. George Wittgraf
Daniel B. Denning, Parade Director

Armed Forces Parade Committee
Major General Donald C. Hilbert, USA
Brigadier General Julius F. Johnson, USA
Mr. Thomas Groppel
District of Columbia Parade Committee
Sam Jordan
Joseph Yeldel

Salute to the First Lady

Mrs. Potter Stewart, Chairman

Committee
The Honorable Jeanie Austin
Mrs. Wallace Boyd
Mrs. Prescott Bush, Sr.
Mrs. John E. Chapoton
Mrs. Masten Childers
The Honorable Margaret Hance
Mrs. Willard Heminway
Mrs. Bobby Holt
Mrs. J. Howard Johnson
Ms. Deborah Leighton
Mrs. William McKenzie
Mrs. DeWitt Neighbors
Mrs. James Shelley Percy
Mrs. Marvin Pierce
Mr. Don Rhodes
Mrs. Jonathan Sloat
Mrs. Stephen M. Studdert
The Honorable Margaret Chase Smith
Mr. Jack Steele

Entertainment
American Boys Choir
Bruce Boxleitner
Duke Ellington School of Performing Arts
Fort Bend Boys Choir
The Gatlin Brothers
Charlton Heston

Houston Symphony Orchestra
Cheryl Ladd
Maguire Sisters
Mora Ariaga Mariachis
National Symphony Orchestra
Sandi Patti
Preservation Hall Jazz Band

Vice Presidential Reception

Mr. and Mrs. William R. Neale, Co-Chairmen

Committee
Mr. and Mrs. Robert Allen
Mr. and Mrs. Allen Autry
The Honorable and Mrs. Earl Baker
The Honorable and Mrs. Howard H. Baker, Jr.
Mr. and Mrs. J. Patrick Barrett
Mr. Lee Beaman
Mr. Robert Bennet
The Honorable and Mrs. Ed Bethune
Mr. and Mrs. Henny Billingsly
Mr. Larry Bird
Mr. Allen Brass
Mr. and Mrs. David Brennan
Mr. and Mrs. Joe Briggs
Mr. and Mrs. Alex P. Courtelis
The Honorable and Mrs. Paul Coverdale
Ms. Alexandra de Borchgrave
Ms. Alice Dolan
Ms. Bev Dolan
The Honorable and Mrs. Pierre S. du Pont, IV
Mr. and Mrs. Gordon Durnil
Mr. and Mrs. Daniel F. Evans, Jr.
Mr. and Mrs. Fred Fielding
Mr. and Mrs. Brook Firestone
Mr. and Mrs. David Fitzgerald
The Honorable and Mrs. Emory Folmar
Mr. and Mrs. Robert Gable
Mr. and Mrs. Bruce Gelb
The Honorable Barry Goldwater
Mr. and Mrs. Steven Gould
Mr. and Mrs. Alan "Punch" Green, Jr.
Mr. Alan Harnish
Father Theodore M. Hesburgh
Mr. and Mrs. Dick Hickman
Mr. Jim Hines
The Honorable Marjorie Holt
Mr. and Mrs. Tim Hubbard
Mr. Mark Hughes
Mr. and Mrs. Ray Hutchison
Mr. and Mrs. William J. Hybl
The Honorable and Mrs. Lee Jackson
The Honorable and Mrs. William Janklow
Mr. F. Edward Johnson
Mr. and Mrs. Celes King, III
Mr. and Mrs. Thomas Kyhos
Ms. Cheryl Ladd
The Honorable and Mrs. Jack Lawton, Jr.
Mr. and Mrs. E. Pat Manual
Mr. and Mrs. Dee Margo
Mr. William McCormick
Mr. Doug McKorkindale
Mr. and Mrs. Tommy Merickel
Mr. and Mrs. Ron Migrant
The Honorable and Mrs. Robert Mosbacher
The Honorable and Mrs. Louie B. Nunn
Mr. and Mrs. John Palmer
Mr. and Mrs. Robert W. Parker
Mr. and Mrs. L. Brooks Patterson
Mr. and Mrs. John Petersen
Mr. Gregg Petersmeyer
Mr. Ed Pratt
Mr. and Mrs. Scott Probasco
The Honorable and Mrs. Donald Rumsfeld
Mr. and Mrs. John Ryder
Mr. and Mrs. Karl Samuelian
Mr. and Mrs. James Schlosser
Mr. and Mrs. Peter F. Secchia
Mr. and Mrs. Clarence Smith
Mr. and Mrs. Roger Staubach
Mr. and Mrs. Vic Stelly
Mr. and Mrs. Jack Stephens
Mr. and Mrs. Patrick F. Taylor
Mr. and Mrs. Robert E. Thomas
Mr. and Mrs. Paul E. Thornbrugh
Mr. and Mrs. Michael Unhjem
Mr. and Mrs. A. D. Van Meter
Mr. John Vardeman
The Honorable and Mrs. Caspar Weinberger
Mr. and Mrs. Joel C. Williams, Jr.
Mr. and Mrs. George W. Wittgraf
Mr. and Mrs. Dalton Woods
Mr. Fuzzy Zoeller

Entertainment
Naptown Jazz Quintet

Photo Credits

Inaugural Book Staff from left to right: Donald E. Rauner, Karen Martinez, Michael Fones, F. C. Duke Zeller, Mary Kearney, Suzanne Bertain Todorovic with baby George (who couldn't wait for Inauguration Day), Barbara A. Cebuhar, Clyde Linsley, Timothy P. O'Neill, Charles E. Lahey, III and Dolores Weiss. Not pictured: Carl S. Anthony, Suzanne Chase, Arnold Drapkin, Jean Fitzgibbon, Byron Kennard, Sydney Leach, Brandi Sullivan.

Inaugural Book Credits

Director and Editor-in-Chief:
F. C. Duke Zeller

Deputy Director and Managing Editor:
Barbara Cebuhar

Associate Editor: Timothy P. O'Neill

Production Manager: Donald E. Rauner

Marketing Manager and Legal Counsel:
Michael Fones

Administration: Bobbie Assure, Robert Berry, Suzanne Bertain, Christine Cobb, William Coyle, Jr., Jacquie Faquer, Jean Fitzgibbon, Mark Ozanick, Betty Priola, William Pugh, David White

Editorial Staff: Maureen Rodgers Amuso, Scott Brown, Suzanne Chase, Pattie Cinnelli, Mary Kearney, Charles E. Lahey, III, Karen Martinez, Brandi Sullivan, Liz Traver and Dolores Weiss

Director of Photography: Arnold Drapkin

Contributing Writers: Kenneth Adelman, Carl Sferrazza Anthony, Warren Burger, Lynne Cheney, Victor Gold, Byron Kennard, Sydney Leach, Clyde Linsley, Timothy P. O'Neill, F. C. Duke Zeller

Inaugural Photographers: JoAnn Amos, Terry Arthur, Terry Ashe, Senator Howard Baker, Susan Biddle, William Cafer, Jerome Delay, Sal DiMarco, Arnold Drapkin, David Drapkin, Ashton Graham, Peter Grant, Mark Higbie, Richard Hofmeister, Peter Kolk, Charles E. Lahey, III, Marty LaVor, Eric Long, Bill Luster, Laurie Minor, Carl Mydans, Kim Nielson, Dane Penland, Carol Powers, Steven Purcell, Marilyn Quayle, Ben Quayle, Corinne Quayle, Tucker Quayle, Alexander Rogers, Karl Schumacher, Diane Stebbins, George Tames, Jessica Thompson, Ron Thompson, Jeff Tinsley, David Valdez, Rick Vargas and Dolores Weiss

Photographic Research: Carl S. Anthony, Helen Casey, Karen Martinez

Design: Frost & Associates

Photography Editors: John Cullather, David Johnson, Karen Martinez, Carole McKay, Don Rauner, Helen Casey

Layout/Final Artwork: Donning Publishing

Printing: Walsworth Publishing

Photo Lab: Dodge Color

The Inaugural Book could not have been produced without the tremendous contribution and professionalism of the following individuals representing the Eastman Kodak Company:

Dennis Kless, Manager Special Events
James Hawkins, Manager Public Relations
Carolyn Jackson, Kodalux, Plant General Manager

Acknowledgements:

With grateful appreciation to the following individuals who contributed immeasurably to the production of this book:

Don Abrahams, Heritage Publishers
Carl Apollonio, Crown Publishing, Inc./ Orion Books
Denise Balzano, The White House
Eric Bing, Huckaby and Associates
Major Raymond H. Blummel, Armed Forces Inaugural Committee
Dennis Brack, Black Star
Philip Brooks, National Archives
David Cohn, Collins Publishing
Herb Collins, Smithsonian Institution
Michael Fiur, The Bicentennial of the Inauguration of George Washington
Carl Frank, Wiley, Rein and Fielding
Alixe Glen, The White House
Dale Gold
Anne Hathaway, The White House
Captain Gail Hayes, Armed Forces Inaugural Committee
Rick Hohlt, U.S. League of Savings Institutions
Stan Huckaby, Huckaby and Associates
Leann Jackson, Good Impressions Printing Co.
Maurice Johnson, Senate Press Gallery

Stanley Kayne, Picture Department, *Time Magazine*
John A. Kelly
Kent Larsen, The Commission on the Bicentennial of the American Constitution
Hal Leaman, Good Impressions Printing Co.
Library of Congress, Still Photo Division
Felix Lowe, Smithsonian Institution Press
Ron Mann, Boeing Aerospace
William McCarthy, President, International Brotherhood of Teamsters
Janet McConnell, White House Photo Office
Dirk Miller, White House Photo Office
Set Momjian
Joyce Natalchyn, The White House
Les Novitsky, The White House
Dr. Clete Pride, The National Geographic Society
Terry Redmond, Carlson Promotion Group
Don Rhodes, The White House
Fred Sainz, The White House
Michael Ruehling, House Rules Committee
Louis Slovinsky, Time, Inc.
Mary Ternes, The Martin Luther King Public Library
Ron and Jessica Thompson, Nikon, Inc.
Chuck Timanus, The Commission for the Bicentennial of the American Constitution
Ron Trowbridge, The Commission for the Bicentennial of the American Constitution
Ben Turner, William D. Harris and Associates, Inc.
Uniphoto
Lynn Urbanski, Collins and Clarke
U.S. Department of State, Office of Protocol
Ben Van Hook, The Louisville Courier Journal
Vireo Photo Agency
James Wallace, Smithsonian Office of Photography
Lynn West, Wiley, Rein and Fielding
Barry Zorthian, Alcalde, O'Bannon, Rousselot and Wahlquist